ADVANCE PRAISE

At a time when the last survivors of World War II are leaving us—
when the horror of the Holocaust is passing from living memory
into history—Rabbi Romberg does an invaluable service in vividly
recreating the life of one of its heroes, Richard Stern. A truly
remarkable man, Stern somehow managed to win both the Iron
Cross fighting as a patriotic German in World War I and, after he
and his family suffered terrible oppression and loss under the
Nazis, a Silver Star fighting for the Americans in World War II.
The life story of Rabbi Romberg's Uncle Richard stands as a
monument to fortitude, bravery, love and, in the end, our never-
dying hope for the brotherhood of the human race.

**Michael Hirsh, senior correspondent and deputy news editor,
Foreign Policy Magazine**

A powerful story of courage and resilience in the face of
unimaginable odds. Romberg excavates and reconstructs Richard
Stern's life as a German infantryman during the First World War, as
a victim of Nazi persecution in the 1930s, and then as a U.S. soldier

during the Allied liberation of Nazi-occupied Europe. The result is a poignant narrative of betrayal and redemption. Parts of this story take one's breath away.

Michael Geheran, author of *Comrades Betrayed: Jewish World War I Veterans under Hitler*

In this anything-but-ordinary intimate account, Jack Romberg presents the story of his uncle Richard Stern, perhaps the only individual to receive both the Iron Cross from Germany and Silver Star from the United States. At once a poignant family memoir and trenchant history, the book weaves the impressions of a young boy with the great events that shaped German Jewry as the Nazis came to power. Capturing the themes of persecution, resistance, and renewal, Romberg successfully raises up the importance of standing for the norms of basic respect, truthfulness, and equality for all as the bedrock of reasonably just societies. Launched from a single photograph of a proud German Jew protesting the corrosion of his democratic Germany, Romberg's personal account reminds us of the importance of standing with those who have the courage to speak truth to power. He has written a beautiful and compelling story that transcends his own family experience and the events that would transform the Jewish people in mid-20th century. It could not be more important for or relevant to our present moment.

Andrew Rehfeld, Ph.D. President, Professor of Political Thought, Hebrew Union College-Jewish Institute of Religion, *Cincinnati-Los Angeles-New York-Jerusalem*

A Doorway to Heroism by W. Jack Romberg is a remarkable recounting of the story of Richard Stern, aka Uncle Richard. Through the course of much research, Romberg has put together the story of his German-Jewish family and specifically his Uncle Richard, who is a heroic figure, not only because he was guided by an unshakeable moral compass but also because he cared deeply for those around him, doing everything in his power to be a force for good. Romberg's thorough investigation of his uncle's story, and ultimately that of his whole family, is an important reminder that there are individuals among us who, even in the face of great personal danger, stand up for what is right. This book invites us in to learn about a hero who should be studied and celebrated. Romberg tells a compelling story as he generously shares his family's history. This volume is a worthy read and fills in some blanks in the existing literature about German-Jewish history.

Rabbi Hara Person, Chief Executive of Central Conference of American Rabbis

There are many amazing stories of German-Jewish refugees joining the U.S. military to fight in World War II. Even amongst these, Richard Stern's story is extraordinary. The journey of "Uncle Richard" from German WWI hero to protester of Nazi policy to American recipient of the Silver Star as a sergeant in his mid-forties is described powerfully showing us both Stern's remarkable life and the warm family connection of Rabbi Romberg.

Michael Rugel, Director of Programs and Content, National Museum of American Jewish Military History

A DOORWAY TO HEROISM

A DECORATED GERMAN-JEWISH SOLDIER WHO BECAME AN AMERICAN HERO

W. JACK ROMBERG

ap

ISBN 9789493231498 (paperback)

ISBN 9789493231511 (hardback)

ISBN 9789493231504 (ebook)

Publisher: Amsterdam Publishers, The Netherlands

info@amsterdampublishers.com

A Doorway to Heroism is Book 15 in the series:

Holocaust Survivor True Stories WWII

Copyright © W. Jack Romberg, 2021

Cover picture: Richard Stern standing in the door of his store protesting the Nazi boycott of Jewish businesses on April 1, 1933. This picture is in numerous museums in Germany. Next to him is a Nazi SA soldier.

CONTENTS

INTRODUCTION

Almost every family has a member with an unusual story. Some are entertaining, some funny, and some have great influence over the rest of the family. What is rare are stories of lives with tremendous impact beyond the family. This is a story of one such life—the life of Richard Stern: decorated German soldier in World War I, Jewish resister in Germany during Hitler's reign of terror, Silver-Star-decorated US Army soldier, and the savior and unifier of a diverse family.

Both of my parents and their families were German-Jewish refugees who arrived in the United States in the latter part of the 1930s. Richard Stern, my father's uncle who raised him, was the most impactful member of the Stern family from 1928 until the late 1940s. He was the one sibling of six who tried to make sure all family members stood by each other instead of engaging in silly arguments, regardless of any circumstance. He absorbed responsibility for family members, despite it ending the path of life he would have preferred. Most significantly, after arriving safely in New York City, he did anything possible to assist relatives stuck in Europe even during the violence of World War II. This included working to help them immigrate to the United States, despite his own lack of money and his need to get established in America. He was exceptionally dedicated to his extended family, including in-laws brought in through his cousin's marriage. Much of the family saw Richard Stern as the most unique, caring member.

What made Richard Stern truly extraordinary, however, were the actions he took beyond his commitment to the family. Perhaps most notable was his act of heroism in the American army in World War II, during a difficult battle in Italy for which he was awarded the Silver Star. It was an action that received bursts of publicity in New York City—articles in numerous newspapers and at least two presentations on the radio, one using a famous actor to portray him in the battle story. He certainly was an unusual soldier for the American army. Exempt from being drafted because of his age, Richard Stern insisted on joining anyway. His unit was an engineering battalion forced to participate in the battle. He had served in the German army in World War I, making him a prior enemy of the American military. It was his personal history and dedication that drove him on the path to become a hero in World War II for the side he once fought against.

Richard Stern was strongly dedicated to his Jewish community. He was a strong supporter of the democratic principles of the German Weimar Republic. He was strong in his opposition to Nazism. Politically, he was a liberal, dedicated to all citizens' entitlement to civil rights. So, when Hitler came to power at the beginning of 1933, Stern felt it was his responsibility, as a decorated German-Jewish war veteran, to protest against the Nazi Party's first official suppressive act against the Jewish community. His choice was unusual for the Jewish community.

In his home city of Cologne, which had one of the largest Jewish communities in Germany, he was the only Jewish person to stage a protest during the April 1, 1933 boycott of Jewish businesses. While the persecution of German Jews kept growing substantially over the next few years, Richard Stern was not sure what to do next for the family members he had brought under his umbrella of responsibility, or even for himself. In the 1930s, he was experiencing the start of the Holocaust. He had fears, yet he pushed forward in numerous ways, finally arranging for himself, his sister Martha, and her son Rudi to immigrate to the United States. Though not traveling together, they all got out of Germany before the war broke out on September 1, 1939.

The story of Richard Stern needs to be told. We have just passed the 75th anniversary of the end of World War II. Most of those veterans are gone, as are most survivors of the Holocaust. Their stories should be preserved, especially those as unique as Richard Stern's. How many American soldiers served the opposing army in World War I, let alone as decorated German soldiers? How many German war veterans then actively opposed the Nazis in the 1930s? How many Jews, after making it safely out of Germany, decided they had to get into the American army to fight Nazi Germany? How many were awarded for heroism?

Richard Stern's history is not only unique for World War II but also unique in the history of the Holocaust. A framed picture of his protest against the Nazis is displayed in numerous museums in Germany. A short version of his story had been taught to German high school students for a few decades as part of their education about the Holocaust. Today, numerous museums and archivists desire the full story of Richard Stern, as they acknowledge it is quite unique. In November of 2018, an Israeli newspaper, *Yedioth Ahronoth*, shared a story about Uncle Richard. In January of 2020, CNN published an article about him for Holocaust Memorial Day. It was read all over the world.

As the article states, Richard Stern was technically my great uncle, but in emotional reality, he was my grandfather. I knew him until he died when I was a bit over 13 years old. I had numerous experiences with him, staying at his home and hearing stories he would tell me. This story of Uncle Richard's life includes my personal experiences, put into the context of his lifelong history. My dad had, and now I have, most of Uncle Richard's documents from his early life, World War I, the 1930s, a large number of letters he wrote or received, and original newspaper articles written about him.

It is important to know key elements of German history to

understand the context of the Stern family's feelings and actions. It is important to know key elements of German-Jewish history to understand the development of the Holocaust beyond simply what Hitler and the Nazi Party did in the 1930s. This book ties Richard Stern's and his family's life to relevant German and German-Jewish history by utilizing historical sources along with Richard Stern's documents and many family letters. In addition, the Katz family, who connected to the Stern family through marriage, experienced situations very connected to Uncle Richard's life.

In today's political and social environment, many people are posting on social media their belief of our country's divisiveness being comparable to the situation in Germany that resulted in the rise of Hitler in Germany. One purpose of this book is to use the Stern family's experience to present the segments of German and German-Jewish history that can be related to how some people view the changing of our country. Everyone can judge for themselves how true that is. While antisemitism is certainly still present in today's world, a moving parallel is between the long history of Jews in Germany and African Americans in the United States. Chapter 2, which tells the story of Uncle Richard's ancestors in the 19th century, also relates the consistency of antisemitism even after the emancipation of the Jewish people in Germany. A purpose specifically for Uncle Richard's biography is to inspire us on how to stand up to prevent dystopia from becoming reality.

It is relevant for the American people to read Uncle Richard's story. It teaches a number of key points, beginning with how we should relate to and care about family and friends. His experience as a protester against the Nazis could be seen in the context of peaceful civil rights protests still happening today but in the context of what life would be like if our government descended into a more authoritarian form. His story as a soldier in World War II is not only unique in his service but also unique in how his life led him to his desire to serve in the American army, despite being exempt from the draft because of his age.

Perhaps most important, to read the story of Richard Stern is to understand how he approached all aspects of life, whether in flourishing or depressing times, whether in personal or public issues. His manners of living, caring, and acting are exemplary even today. It is time to share them widely.

1

SITTING BULL'S FAVORITE CHAIR

It was June of 1960, a few weeks after I turned six years old. My family had lived in Fairmont, West Virginia, for five years, and Uncle Richard was visiting us. He took me on a walk, something he always loved to do. We lived on a dirt road that went up and around a long hill. There were houses only on one side of the road, as the other side was a little valley with a forest and a creek. Several houses up from us, the road curved sharply to continue up the hill. At the curve was an entrance to a meadow placed on a sloped part of the hill, where I would often go sledding during winter. There was a line of trees along the edge of the meadow leading back into the forest.

After going up the dirt road to where it curved around the hill, we went into the meadow, walking along the edge of the forest. Uncle Richard then grew a serious expression on his face. He told me we were searching for Indians because it was very important to talk with them. He said to watch for a path through the forest that would lead to an Indian settlement. We did not find that path. Instead, we found a large, thickly upholstered chair filled with rips and holes. Obviously, someone had disposed of it in the forest. As we looked at this junky chair, my uncle said it was something significant.

"Jackie," he said, "this was Sitting Bull's favorite chair." He then concluded that the Indians must have moved, and we would not find them, so it was time to walk back home.

My times with Uncle Richard always felt different than those spent with other relatives. Much later, I would learn the depth of his difference, that he was a man whose moment of courage in the face of Nazism was unique among German Jews, and that he became a hero in the US Army during World War II.

What do I mean by a unique relative? Richard Stern was my dad's uncle, so technically, he was my great-uncle. Dad's mother, who I called Nana, was Martha Romberg née Stern. Richard Stern was her brother. Dad's parents divorced by the time he was three years old. Uncle Richard's and Nana's father, Markus, had Dad and Nana living in his house. When Markus died in 1928, Uncle Richard became my dad's legal guardian. So, at 28 years old, he took responsibility for his sister and her son, Rudi, my dad. Uncle Richard grew so close to my dad through his childhood that he looked at him as his true son. He saw my brother Len and me as his grandsons, and I saw him as my grandfather. That was certainly somewhat unique.

Both of my parents' families were German-Jewish refugees. My mom's family landed in New York on March 25, 1936. I called my mom's mother "Oma" (Grandma) and her father "Opa" (Grandpa). As a little boy, I thought I called Dad's father "Uncle Richard" because my mom's father's name was "Opa." It was more than his name that made Uncle Richard unique. Even in my early childhood, I sensed something different about him. In June of 1960, I was excited because Uncle Richard visited us in Fairmont for the first time.

My parents, Ellen and Rudi Romberg, were married on February 22, 1953 in New York, about seven months after they met at the Takanassee Hotel, a popular resort for German-Jewish immigrants on vacation in the Catskills. Dad's mom, Martha, interfered nastily in many of Dad's relationships over the years. She constantly pushed him to let her go along on his dates with women in the late 1940s. In 2018 I actually met a woman who broke up with

Dad because of that. Strangely, Dad was engaged to two other women before meeting my mom. In a letter at the end of World War II, Martha expressed her opposition to Dad's first engagement in 1945. Her attitude toward my mom was no exception. After they were married, Mom wanted to have each family come over to see their new apartment in Forest Hills, Queens. It was too small to receive both families at the same time, as Mom entertained by cooking for her guests. She invited her parents first. Martha resented that she was not included, beginning a series of nasty exchanges in which she said terrible things about my mom's parents.

Mom heard about Martha going to Dad's furniture factory in New York to complain about her. Martha did it with so much acrimony, she would hit her head against the wall. By August of 1953, Mom was ready to file for divorce, but Dad convinced her not to leave him. She became pregnant with me shortly afterward. That led to the next conflict. Martha told Dad that she, not his wife, had to be the beneficial receiver of his GI insurance as a war veteran. Martha felt her financial well-being had to be Dad's priority. That was understandable, given her struggle to reach economic stability as a German-Jewish refugee arriving before the war. It was the pushy way she went about it that created conflict.

In August of 1953, after Dad convinced Mom not to file for divorce, Uncle Richard came to their apartment to talk with Mom. He asked her to capitulate at least a little to Martha. Mom asked him not to interfere. She did not dislike Uncle Richard, but she could not understand why he would ask her to give in to Martha without any explanation of her attitude. Uncle Richard could not share with Mom the reason for Martha's constant antagonistic feelings and actions. At that time, only two people knew Martha's true, full history.

Sometime in 1922, when Martha was 21 years old, she met Walter Romberg. Probably a couple of years before they met, Walter had an affair with a woman who bore a little boy who died in 1925 at a very young age in a street accident. Walter and Martha got married on March 9, 1923. It is clear this was a "shotgun" wedding, as Dad was born on July 11, 1923. Apparently, Walter asked Martha to take responsibility for caring for the little boy he fathered through the woman of his earlier affair. She refused. In a letter to Dad written May 9, 1943, Uncle Richard tried to teach Dad the importance of clear thinking and safe sex. Describing Martha's experience with Walter, he informed Dad that his biological father had led a very unsteady life, and that Martha ended up with an ongoing infection transmitted to her by Walter. This caused constant discomfort that amplified her already short temper. The most important part of Uncle Richard's letter was that no one, not even her other siblings, knew the full cause of her difficulty. He insisted Dad must maintain the secrecy, stressing that he does not tell his mom that he had learned the cause of her problems.

My mom did not realize in 1953 how Uncle Richard was trying to bridge the difficult gap between the woman his nephew Rudi loved, and Rudi's mom, Uncle Richard's sister. In 1955 the situation was somewhat resolved. An economic development authority approached Dad with an offer to transfer his furniture factory from New York to Fairmont, West Virginia. They offered financial benefits as part of their attempt to diversify the state's economy from predominantly coal mining. Dad accepted the offer, so when we moved, the connection between Mom and Martha became distant. Around the same time, Uncle Richard and the woman he married only a few years earlier moved from New York to Allentown, Pennsylvania, to take advantage of a new business opportunity.

We lived in Fairmont and would often drive a long distance to visit Oma's and Opa's house in the Bronx. I would live with them for a summer stretch and often go up for Chanukah in December. On the way, we would stop at Uncle Richard's house in Allentown to visit him for a couple of days before continuing to New York. Uncle Richard had something special to give me when we arrived. Whether we stopped first at his little grocery store or his home, he always had a few silver dollars for me, some dating back to the 1870s. Those silver dollars were the beginning of a coin collection I have had my whole life.

It was through those visits I got to know Uncle Richard. I enjoyed being with him, even though there were times he could be a little rough. For example, I was a terrible eater at dinner, and I got upset when he scolded me because I hated to eat vegetables. As a child, I saw those moments as meanness and not about my health. Yet, I saw the tears in his eyes when our visit ended every time we said goodbye. I felt the love in his heart despite some moments of scolding. I respected him, and together, we had many fun activities and interactions. I was excited to hear he was finally coming to visit us in Fairmont, believing he was visiting to have a fun time with me. I had no idea about the real reason he was coming.

In the middle of 1959, my nana was diagnosed with cancer. The treatments gave her temporary pain relief but no permanent cure. I loved Nana. Whenever I stayed with Oma and Opa in the Bronx, I would usually spend a day with Nana. Her job was to take care of a little girl about my age, so she would take me to play with her. Sometimes Dad and I would go to her apartment to sleep over for a night, and Nana always made one of my favorite treats, home-cooked chocolate pudding. While she was nasty to Mom, she only treated me with love. So, I knew nothing about her relationship with my mom. Even at five years old, I was sad to hear she was in the hospital.

Uncle Richard constantly took a bus from Allentown to New York, helping her get to treatments, and later visit her in the hospital. He sent letters to Dad with reports on her condition. In the spring of 1960, Mom and Dad visited Nana in the hospital. She knew that death was close. While lying in the hospital bed, Nana finally apologized to Mom, knowing she had mistreated her. She stressed to Dad he must always stay with Mom, and she praised how wonderful Mom was. She died on May 16, 1960, two weeks before I turned six years old. That is when Uncle Richard decided to come to Fairmont to spend time with our family.

Arriving in mid-June, he stayed for over a week, sleeping on a bed in my baby brother Len's room. He wanted to reboot his relationship with Mom, a typical example of his actions to heal family conflicts. While with us, he did not focus on analyzing prior situations, the problems between Mom and Martha. Instead, he worked on getting to know Mom. A few years later, when we moved near him in Allentown, Uncle Richard and Mom became very close. He always took her side in her arguments with Dad, saying, "Rudi, Ellen is right!" He had never learned how to drive, so he preferred Mom to drive him instead of his own wife or Dad when he needed to go somewhere.

Of course, the other reason Uncle Richard wanted to be with us in Fairmont was to spend time with his grandsons, Len and me. As a six-year-old, I believed he preferred to spend time with me more than with a brother who was only a year-and-a-half old. Each time I visited him in Allentown, Uncle Richard and I would take fun walks around his neighborhood. Typically, he made up some story about what we were seeing that made me laugh. Now, I wanted to do the same with him in our neighborhood in Fairmont. It was different from Allentown. Fairmont was small, and West Virginia a state of mountains.

Uncle Richard was really interested in stories about Native Americans. He had grown up reading books by Karl May, an author whose books were popular among young Germans from the end of the 19th century until almost the mid-20th century. Our house in West Virginia was in a much less developed area than Uncle Richard's house in Allentown. Between the dirt road, the forest, creek, and meadow, it felt like we were on the edge of a wilderness —at least to me. Having spent summers living with my Oma and Opa in the Bronx and having visited and taken walks in Allentown with Uncle Richard, I felt a huge difference in the atmospheres of those living areas. I was excited when Uncle Richard told me one day that our activity was to take a walk beyond the road into the meadow to look for an "Indian" settlement.

First, we played on the swing set in our yard. Then, knowing I was waiting for it, he said it was time for our walk. We went up the dirt road to enter the meadow. Uncle Richard and my Oma and Opa all had heavy German accents, which I actually thought was cool to hear. While we walked that day in West Virginia, Uncle Richard would suddenly stop and say in his German accent, "I shmell money!" I asked where and he told me to look around. On the ground would be a penny, a nickel, or a dime. I would pick it up to show him. He would say I should keep it, since I found it. A few years later, when we lived in Allentown, I saw him do the same thing when walking with my brother. However, by nine years old, I knew Uncle Richard was dropping the coins for us, but I did not tell Len.

After hearing his comment on Sitting Bull, I recognized, even at six years old, this was Uncle Richard's humor. What I did not know was the complexity of his life. I had no idea that he once had friends in Germany who admired his humor. I knew he loved our family but had no clue how his life had been dedicated to helping anyone and everyone in his family, no matter how distant a relative. I had not yet known what he experienced as a Jew growing up in Germany, and how he dealt with the Nazis' rise to power in 1933, of his involvement in politics to fight for civil rights. I was still to learn that he had fought for Germany in World War I and for the United States in World War II. I had no idea how he had to give up a successful business because of the Nazi persecution of Jews or of the impact the Holocaust had on him. I had not yet seen the famous picture of him protesting against the Nazis in 1933, which today is displayed in numerous museums throughout Germany. I had no idea he was a hero in many ways that word could be defined.

When Uncle Richard visited us at our West Virginia home in June of 1960, I knew almost nothing about the reality of his life, even though it was still unfolding during the years we were together. I knew almost nothing about the Stern family.

For many years, Dad had a photograph of a house called "Villa Stern" hanging in his office. I did not know where it was or about its role in Uncle Richard's life. As a little boy who had just finished kindergarten, I had no idea why my family had emigrated from Germany or that the Stern family's history began at a time when Jews were still not emancipated and allowed to assimilate into the general German society. I had no idea he was the descendant of a man who played a significant role in a Jewish community in the early to the mid-19th century.

I would know Uncle Richard until he was almost 69 years old, but he had lived for 55 years before I was born, and he rarely spoke to me about his earlier life. It was only when I became older and studied German history in college that I began to understand what his experiences might have truly been. That is when I realized I must learn more about Uncle Richard's life.

Richard Stern and Jack Romberg in Fairmont, West Virginia (June 1960)

2

JEWISH EMANCIPATION

Uncle Richard's great-grandfather, Seligmann Stern, was born in Harburg, Bavaria, in 1793. He lived for an amazing 84 years, not merely establishing the Stern family's presence in the Rhineland, in the German state of Prussia, but dedicating much of his life to building the basis for the Jewish community in a county not far from Cologne that contained a group of smaller towns. Seligmann Stern's life parallels a constantly changing Jewish situation in the Prussian state and the German Reich. His life set an exemplary standard of a caring, successful German Jew for his descendants to admire and try to emulate. Seligmann Stern's accomplishments and dedication to the Jewish community must have been an inspiration to Uncle Richard.

He was born before German rulers officially emancipated the Jewish people. In 1812, the Prussian king, Frederick William III, finally approved an edict emancipating Jews and formally recognizing them as full citizens.[1] This was not of Prussian societal origin but the result of Napoleon's conquest of the German states; just three years later, the edict was suspended after Napoleon's defeat.[2] The evolving hatred of Jews in the early 19th century was not so much against Jews who were aliens in Germany, or traditional observers of Judaism, but those in the Jewish middle class who were trying to assimilate into overall Prussian society.[3] Through the 19ᵗʰ into the 20ᵗʰ century, many Jews decided to strengthen their identity as Germans by converting to Christianity. Yet, still, those who converted from Judaism experienced antisemitic hatred even if their family had converted a generation or two before they were born. This attitude laid the groundwork for the racist form of antisemitism that developed in the 20ᵗʰ century.[4] Seligmann Stern's assimilation centered on friendships with non-Jewish Germans. While he might not have been Orthodox in his religious observance, he cared deeply about Judaism and Jewish communities. He trained to become a teacher of Jewish students. It is not clear if he taught secular subjects to Jewish children as well, since they were not allowed to attend schools with German Christians. He left his hometown at the age of 20 to take his first position as a schoolteacher in Badorf, a town in the Rhineland, where he taught for four years.

In 1818, Seligmann moved to Niedermendig, where he joined the army for one year, common among Jews in Germany who were eager to demonstrate their patriotism.[5] During the 19ᵗʰ century, German Jews tried hard to show their countrymen that they were patriotic Germans to try to counter anti-Jewish hatred. Seligmann's service in the army set a precedent for the Stern family descendants over the next hundred years, which was particularly important during World War I.

After his year in the army, Seligmann taught in two more towns before ending up in Weilerswist, Prussia, a town not far from Cologne, arriving in 1822. Constant relocation was typical of young Jewish teachers in that time period as they searched for a community that could at least provide a basic salary. During his two-year contract teaching in Weilerswist, Seligmann met and fell in love with Helena Heumann, who was twenty-two years old. She lived in Friesheim, a nearby town, with her widowed mother. After his contract in Weilerswist ended, he moved to Friesheim, where Helena's mother allowed him to move into her house so he could be close to his fiancée. Seligman and Helena got married in 1826. Matthias Curth, the mayor of Friesheim, issued this statement about Seligmann Stern settling there:

> "Seligmann Stern was staying in Weilerswist in September 1824 and taught children for one year. He became very engaged in local affairs of Jews. Based on his good credentials and good ratings from various mayors, I gave him permission to stay. During the last months he lived with the widow Heumann; he was never engaged in commerce like the other local Jews did; he traveled home now and then to visit his relatives and took some of his inheritance in order to financially support the widow Heumann. He courted the daughter of the widow Heumann for two years and married her five months ago; he became the husband of the daughter of the widow Heumann, where he lived and worked as a servant before. Based on his behavior he is accepted by me, the mayor, and also by the entire community."[6]

This quote from Mayor Curth confirms Seligmann's commitment to the Jewish community as well as his positive interactions with the rest of the Friesheim community. It also shows how dedicated he was to his family.

If Seligmann Stern met and fell in love with Helena Heumann in 1823, then moved in with her widowed mother in 1824, why did their marriage not occur until 1826? According to the book *Heimat an der Erft* by Heidi and Cornelius Bormann, he was ready to marry Helena in March of 1824, but could not because he was unable to provide needed documents. He was still a citizen of Bavaria, not Prussia where Friesheim was located. So he traveled to the town of his birth, Harburg. The Bavarian government was willing to issue a release certificate, but only if the Prussian government would assure his acceptance as a Prussian citizen.

Mayor Matthias Curth of Friesheim sent a letter to that area's county commissioner, in Euskirchen, saying that he wanted Seligmann Stern to get the release from Bavaria as he was "a very honest man and well loved by our community."[7] Mayor Curth pushed the Prussian government to provide an acceptance certificate in order for Bavaria to issue the release. The commissioner felt it was something he should not be bothered to do, for his response from September 29, 1824, says, "I note with surprise that you have not considered the law of March 17, 1808, pertaining to the Jewish Ordinance when filing the application on August 31 for the consensus of resettlement of the Israelite Seligmann Stern."[8]

The law he referred to was an anti-Jewish law issued while the Rhineland was still under the rule of France during Napoleon's time as emperor. This law restricted the civil rights of the Jews. They had to change their names from the traditional Jewish structure of the surname being the first name of the head of the family (e.g. Natan ben Moshe—the Hebrew version that literally means Nathan son of Moses ergo Nathan Moses). The law also required Jews to apply to authorities for trading permits, and permission to market and sell items. The Stern family had clearly already done the required name change. While trying to settle into a full, married life in Friesheim, Seligmann was trying to establish a business career. It is significant that the mayor of Friesheim felt so strongly about Seligmann's quality as a human that he was willing to advocate for him against the consistent anti-Jewish realities throughout Germany. The county commissioner in 1824 was either himself antisemitic or felt the Jewish Ordinance made Seligmann's application too complicated to successfully submit.

One of the complications of Seligmann's attempts to change his citizenship from Bavarian to Prussian was tied to his two sisters, Zierle and Besele, who were also trying to change their citizenship from Bavaria to Prussia. On March 2, 1825, the court of Harburg, Bavaria issued this statement to Seligmann Stern:

"It is true that Seligmann Stern received a release certificate from the Royal Bavarian government to resettle in Friesheim, but only under the expressed condition that Stern provides the reception certificate of the relevant authorities. This has not happened. We request that Stern provides these certificates. Regarding the two sisters, it is mandatory for them to be present here in order to manage their assets."[9]

The two sisters were given the deadline of April 22, 1825, to return to Harburg for a meeting with the court to manage their inheritance. It was too short of a time for either sister to comply with that deadline. Seligmann's sister Zierle had only been in Friesheim a few days before going to the town of Deutz near Cologne. A letter sent to the court in Harburg from Friesheim stated she was not able to make the trip back to Harburg. His younger sister, Besele, stayed in Friesheim for several months, but had a child and was also not able to appear in the court by April 22, 1825.[10]

There are no records about how the citizenship issue was resolved for Seligmann's sisters. However, for Seligmann, it stayed unresolved for over two decades. A key question, for which there is no proven answer, is how much this delay for citizenship was based on Prussian antisemitism. By 1841, he had been married for 15 years. He ran a fruit dealership in Friesheim, and his oldest son, Samson, wanted to start learning how to be a glazier. This was all technically not allowed unless Seligmann became a Prussian citizen. His wife, Helena, had given birth to 10 children, but only five had survived. After this stretch of life, there was still no resolution of the old citizenship request. In September of 1841, the current county commissioner and the new mayor of Friesheim tried to resolve the issue by contacting the Prussian government office in Cologne, requesting a trade certificate to legalize Seligmann's position and fulfill the desire of his son. Even then, nothing was resolved.

In 1843, the county commissioner of Friesheim tried one more time, sending this message to the government office, "Seligmann Stern has lived in Friesheim for 20 years; he is the father of 5 children; he is very industrious and has purchased an apartment and his behavior remains impeccable. The question as to whether he can obtain a citizenship certificate is subject to a decision made at a higher level."[11] While it took another five years to even receive a response on this issue, the higher level of the Prussian government finally, in 1848, resolved the issue, as he obtained citizenship and thus finally got the official title of a fruit dealer.

The conclusion of this issue for Seligmann Stern parallels improvement in the overall status of Jews throughout Germany. In 1848, there was an attempt to create a united German Reich that would be a democratic republic. There were political connections between active Jews and liberal Germans, pushing to establish a parliamentary system. This revolution failed, which meant that German Jews still did not get full emancipation. Yet, this event did improve the movement of German Jews towards full citizenship by strengthening the connection between politically active German Jews and certain German parties for the next few decades.[12]

When looking at the positive letters written on his behalf by the mayors of Friesheim and the county commissioners, it is clear that Seligmann Stern was a very popular local person. However, even more significant was his activism on behalf of the Jewish community in the area, which included the towns of Weilerswist, Friesheim, and Erfstadt. During the years he was living in Friesheim, Seligmann was a dominant member of the Jewish community, acting as their speaker and leader. On March 8, 1851, he directed the purchase agreement to establish a Jewish cemetery in Friesheim.[13] By 1865, he bought property in the nearby town of Erfstadt to build a house and established the area's first synagogue behind his house.[14] That synagogue existed until the violent destruction of Jewish synagogues all across Germany during Kristallnacht on November 9, 1938.

Whether it was envy, Seligmann's strong personality, or simply aging, a tension developed between him and the area's Jewish community as he turned 74. His son, Michael Stern, born on March 2, 1835, took over the house in Erfstadt, where the synagogue was located. Seligmann moved out of the area for a brief period but returned and lived with Michael and his family until he died on

January 2, 1877.[15] There is no question that his life of business success, popularity in the general community, and hard work on behalf of the local Jewish community must have inspired the Stern family for the next few generations.

Michael Stern had five sons, Markus, Hermann, Leopold, Moses, and Simon. At some point, each one of these sons left the Friesheim/Wielerswist area to advance their business careers. Hermann and Moses each moved to Essen, Germany, while Leopold and Simon moved to Cologne. Leopold had a successful retail business in Cologne. One of Simon Stern's businesses was real estate development. Markus Stern was likely the last one to move to a larger city. He also was Uncle Richard's father.

Markus Stern was born on October 18, 1861. His wife, Elise Carl, was from Weilerswist. They got married on June 28, 1887, and settled in Weilerswist. Here are their seven children born there:

- Heinrich: born on May 3, 1888
- Richard: born on January 15, 1890, but died at 6 years old
- Thekla: born on July 2, 1892
- Henriette: born on December 9, 1894
- Hilda: born on October 30, 1896
- Richard Felix: born on February 22, 1899 – this is Uncle Richard named for the brother who died in 1896.
- Martha: born on March 11, 1901

Markus Stern worked extremely hard and grew successful, running several businesses, often being employed to do jobs on buildings by the town of Weilerswist. Like his uncle Samson, he was a glass installer, but his initial business was painting. He also ran a seed business. Advertisements from the late 1880s and 1890s show these businesses all existed at the same time. In addition to all these businesses, Markus Stern was also a mortgage provider.

There were few elaborate homes in Weilerswist in the 1890s and not even many buildings of any kind near the train station. The bulk of the land was agricultural. A man by the name of Anton

Zimmermann owned a lot of the undeveloped plots of land. He passed away in 1893, and his children sold the property to Simon Stern, Markus's brother living in Cologne, in March of 1898. Simon and Markus immediately began to build a massive villa on this property.[16] It was two stories, built on a complex plan that featured a high base, a mezzanine floor, and a many-faceted roof featuring a timber framing style. Its style was unique and unknown in the town of Weilerswist. The house became known as "Villa Stern." It was surrounded by gardens, fountains, and a meadow. While the term "villa" was common, Villa Stern was one of the largest and most wholly unique homes in Weilerswist.

This is the house in which Uncle Richard was born. While it is no longer called "Villa Stern," the house still exists today and is owned by the town of Weilerswist. It is considered historic and used as a place to teach children and teenagers music and acting. It is just outside of the shopping area in Weilerswist, right next to the town hall. The house is still impressive. In the summer of 2020, the town council decided to place a plaque on it, honoring Richard Stern and his family.

The rise of business success for the Stern family, particularly Markus, Leopold, and Simon, fits the context of German-Jewish business success by the end of the 19th century. It is not that the Sterns were among the wealthiest of Jewish families. They were not. However, the overall success rate of middle-class Jews had risen to a great degree.[17] The Stern family was part of that rise. There were many improvements for German Jews, yet the presence of antisemitism became more deeply rooted in ways that laid the groundwork for the eventual rise of the Nazi Party decades later.

In 1871, when Markus Stern was a boy of 10, important events would bring great changes to German Jewry. The Franco-Prussian war ran from the middle of 1870 until early 1871. For the most part, German Jews supported the generally accepted cause of the war: French aggression.[18]

"As a soldier I am ready to be mere cannon fodder. For this even a Jew like myself is good enough," wrote Jewish author Berthold Auerbach, reflecting the attitude of many German Jews.[19]

There was indeed an impressive number of Jewish soldiers in the German army. Even more impressive was the number of German-Jewish soldiers who earned the Iron Cross, which was awarded for valor. The actual formation of the first united Germany (German Reich) occurred in January of 1871. As the Franco-Prussian war came to an end, the southern German states, except Austria, became united with the northern states.

In 1871, an emancipation law for the entire German Reich was approved. This law abolished all restrictions on civil and political rights based on "religious differences."[20] This is clearly what German Jews had wanted for almost a century. In addition, a law approved in 1874 permitted mixed civil marriages for the first time in German history.[21] A wide segment of German Jews hoped to achieve greater assimilation, but they did not necessarily promote mixed marriages. But making them legal seemed to indicate that German society was growing more accepting. Indeed, intermarriage increased to over 29 percent by 1915.[22] Even more impactful was the increase of Jewish involvement in politics, in particular the formation and rise of the Social Democratic Party. The SDP pushed for human rights in Germany. This helped German Jews form a Jewish lobby that became the largest representation of Jews in the Reich—the "Union of German Citizens of the Jewish Faith."[23]

There were definitely segments of time in Germany when antisemitic groups shrunk or failed.[24] But the reality was that the hatred of Jews did not fade away. Rather, there were new branches of antisemitism forming in many parts of German society and politics. Before the unity of all the German states, German nationalism was different than after the formation of the Reich. Nationalism had previously centered on unifying the various German states and had been part of movements opposing social and religious prejudice. However, after the Reich was established, German nationalism became "conservative, xenophobic, conformist, and worshipful of militarists who had brought it about."[25] These growing aspects were connected to the rising feeling that Germany was a superior country. It is easy to see how these elements connect to the rise of the Nazi Party in the 1920s. When something went wrong, the Jewish people were the most likely minority to be blamed.

For example, in 1873, when the stock market crashed, tens of thousands of German families suffered deep economic losses. Jews were falsely blamed for enriching themselves at the financial expense of other citizens.[26] The fact that many Jews were stockbrokers inflated this feeling that Jews were immoral and inferior. In addition, many racial versions of antisemitism that had existed only on radical edge groups just a few years earlier now gained popularity. The shocking reality was that, despite the legal and economic assimilation of Jews taking place passively just a few years earlier, the fast eruption of hatred of Jews in the economic crisis illustrated its durability.[27]

The experience of the Stern family throughout the 19th century illustrates several aspects of those years of German-Jewish history. First, I wonder if the Prussian government's constant failure to process Seligmann Stern and his sisters' applications for citizenship changes were connected to limitations because of their status as Jews. Yet, local political leaders in the Friesheim/Weilerswist area were inspired by Seligmann's human decency regardless of his religion. Second, Seligmann's service in the Prussian army occurred during the early years of Jewish expression of patriotism for Germany. Finally, over the course of the 19th century, as Jews became more financially successful, so did the Stern family. As the century came to a close, most of Seligmann's descendants moved to larger German cities, where they had expanded opportunities for success.

By 1900, Markus Stern was the only one of his brothers remaining in the area of Friesheim/Weilerswist. In 1902, his eldest son, Heinrich, had finished elementary and middle school and, at fourteen years old, wanted to go to Cologne to study in a merchandise school and then serve an apprenticeship. A few years later, Heinrich was ready to begin a business and apparently opened a store in Cologne on Krefelder Street. The business sold second-grade, discounted textile products. Markus helped his son start a business and then must have decided to move all of his family to Cologne. Clearly, there were a number of items that had to be sold and concluded in order to move the family.

Markus's brother Simon had assigned to him the power of attorney for selling Villa Stern, along with several other properties he owned in numerous cities. That was signed in April 1906. Markus Stern sold Villa Stern to a veterinarian, August Adolf Jonen, in March of 1907. The seed business was transferred in June of 1907 to Melchior Kirsch. It was popular enough that Marcus Stern and Melchior Kirsch placed this ad in the local newspaper:

Transfer of Seed Business

The seed business that was run by me in Weilerswist was transferred today to Mr Kirsch in Weilerswist. I'd like to thank you all for your trust in my and like to ask you to support my successor in the same fashion.

Respectfully! Marcus Stern

I'd like to join the above declaration of my predecessor and like to ask you to have the same trust in me, as I will conduct the seed business in the same way and I will remain committed to accommodate the wishes and requirements of my customers.

Respectfully! Melchior Kirsch, Kuhlseggen Mill in Weilerswist. Grain, Crop, and Feed business[28]

By the middle of 1907, Markus Stern had moved his family to the growing city of Cologne.

In 1900, the population of Cologne was 372,552. When Markus moved his family there in 1907, it had already grown to 451,134. It would provide much larger business possibilities, one of which he started with his oldest son, Heinrich. In addition to rejoining two of his brothers, Marcus likely welcomed the opportunity to live in a larger Jewish community. As German Jews were rising economically, large city communities were building large, elaborate synagogues. In Cologne, the largest synagogue, Roonstrasse, which the Stern family would join, was built in 1899, the same year that Uncle Richard was born. The Roonstrasse Synagogue was a liberal Jewish synagogue. It is likely that the activity of the Stern family in Judaism, beginning with Seligmann, mirrored active Jews in the liberal Reform movement in Germany. The Roonstrasse Synagogue was tied to the history of the Stern family for the first four decades of the 20th century.

I moved from Fairmont, West Virginia, to Allentown, Pennsylvania, at nine years old, almost the same age as Uncle Richard when he moved to Cologne. My life opened up in ways I could never have imagined, beginning with a significantly larger Jewish community. My education opportunities improved. Being with Uncle Richard deepened my family connections and taught me more about our family history. Cologne was much larger than Allentown, so there is no doubt that the move to Cologne opened a large door of possibilities for Uncle Richard.

Although the Stern family was not Orthodox in religious observance, each generation was dedicated to the Jewish community. Even after settling in Cologne, Uncle Richard must have learned a lot of his family history: their success, dedication to the Jewish people, ability to assimilate with the general German population, and German patriotism. Coming from a small group of towns friendly to German Jews, he felt he would succeed at the same high level as much of his family. He also believed that even though he was a dedicated Jew, he could also have strong connections to his non-Jewish friends and business associates. All these expectations were set by his great-grandfather Seligmann Stern. When Uncle Richard began his life in Cologne, he was on an expected path, which would make his actual future a huge surprise.

Villa Stern in Weilerswist, Germany

Villa Stern in Weilerswist, Germany (2019)

Synagogue built by Seligmann Stern in Freisheim, Germany.
Destroyed during Kristallnacht

1. Elon, p 95
2. Ibidem
3. Idem, p 98
4. Idem, p 99
5. Idem, p 95
6. Bormann, p 247
7. Idem, p 248
8. Ibidem
9. Ibidem
10. Ibidem
11. Idem, p 249
12. Elon, p 179
13. Heimat an der Erft, p 249
14. Ibidem
15. Ibidem
16. Kurten, p 3
17. Elon, p 259
18. Idem, p 202
19. Idem, p 205
20. Idem, p 209
21. Idem, p 225
22. Idem, p 241
23. Idem, p 221
24. Idem, p 199
25. Idem, pp 210-211

26. Idem, p 213
27. Kurten, p 4
28. Idem, p 5

3

THE CHANUKAH MAN

The location of my dad's furniture factory in Fairmont, West Virginia, did not work out well. By the summer of 1963, our family moved to Allentown, Pennsylvania, where Dad found a good place to continue his business. At nine years old, I was excited over how much closer we would be to my oma and opa, who lived in the Bronx. It would be much easier to visit them or for them to visit us. It felt special to live in the same city as Uncle Richard. What I did not know until years later was that Uncle Richard helped our family make the move. He had given my dad five thousand dollars —part of that to cover the costs of resettlement. The balance was to help Dad relocate his furniture manufacturing.

I did know that Uncle Richard loved spending time with my brother, Len, and me. Our first home in Allentown was not a far walk from the Allentown Fairgrounds. It was an older neighborhood, with lots of trees along the road. Our home was a duplex. Shortly after we were settled, Uncle Richard took us on a walk to the Allentown Fair. He took us to see the farm animals, bought us lunch, and paid for us to play all kinds of games. I enjoyed the fair so much that I went every year. Later, after I was married and had two kids of my own, I would drive back to Allentown so my daughters could enjoy the fair. Just like I became enchanted with the Allentown Fair through Uncle Richard, he became enchanted as a child with the *Karneval* of Cologne, which he experienced every year beginning in 1908.

Another event Uncle Richard enjoyed as a little child was the arrival of Chanukah Man (in Yiddish or German, Chanukah Mensch) every year. He was the Jewish version of Santa Claus and a common German-Jewish tradition. I experienced it almost every year as a little boy spending Chanukah in New York with my mom's family. I would attend German-Jewish Chanukah parties. At one party, I was sitting on the Chanukah Man's lap. I looked down at his shoes, recognizing them the same as my dad's. The Chanukah Man (Dad) told me he had met up with my dad in a shoe store.

The Stern family made a big deal out of the Chanukah Man being there for the children. For many years, Uncle Richard was the one who dressed up as the Chanukah Man for his sibling's children. In a letter his sister Martha sent to my dad while he was in the army in 1944, she mentioned how Uncle Richard enjoyed doing this for all of his sisters' children in Cologne years earlier. He loved being the Chanukah Man and wanted to do it for my brother and me. Once we moved to Allentown, he could be ours during Chanukah, the first time in December 1963.

On the first night of Chanukah, Dad said there would be a special surprise. Just after we lit our Chanukah candles and sang *Ma'oz Tzur* (Stronghold of Rock), the doorbell rang, and in walked Chanukah Man carrying gifts. He wore a mask with a beard, a top hat, a *tallis*, and carried a long cane topped with a Jewish star. As a nine-year-old who had experienced this since I was a toddler, I knew that it was really Uncle Richard. My brother Len had never seen a Chanukah Man, so when he walked into our house, Len became so scared he ran upstairs to hide in his bedroom. It took my dad about 10 minutes to convince him that Chanukah Man was safe before getting him back downstairs to receive his gifts.

Moving to a city to join other family members can be special. We had Uncle Richard and his wife, Aunt Hilde. When Uncle Richard moved to Cologne with his parents, the family already there was not just his older brother Heinrich. His oldest sister,

Thekla, at only 15 years old, had moved to Cologne a few months before her parents and siblings to get her first job. Her mom, Elise, had helped her move and get settled. Two of his father's brothers, Simon and Leopold, lived there, so as he grew older, a lot of family was present to bring help, caring, and pleasantness into his life. He was fortunate to have them, as the path of the German nation was already heading in a difficult direction. The development of this Chanukah Man was in a far more complex environment than any child could imagine.

After settling in Cologne with his family in 1907, the next 11 years of Uncle Richard's life were not just about physical growth from childhood to adulthood, but also about living during a volatile time for German Jews and all German citizens. During his childhood, Uncle Richard learned a sense of his country's needs as well as the constantly changing atmosphere affecting the Jewish people. The first year and a half of his adulthood would be spent in the German army during the final stage of World War I, when the country completely fell apart. Like so many German Jews, he felt patriotic toward his country, yet he very much supported the changes that occurred as the war ended and during its aftermath.

While the Germany of almost the first two decades of Uncle Richard's life had an active Reichstag (parliament), the country was a true monarchy. Their kaiser (emperor), Wilhelm II, had taken the throne in 1888. It was his authority to appoint the country's chancellor as well as the full cabinet without the Reichstag's approval.[1] Further, the Reichstag was a parliament with additional limitations. It could not dismiss the cabinet. It could not tell the kaiser whether or not to enter a war. The kaiser's choice was critical. Also, it had little power in managing the nation's budget.[2]

In 1909, Kaiser Wilhelm II had to choose a new chancellor and selected Theobald von Bethmann-Hollweg.[3] At this point, German society was already extremely obsessed with the military. This not only influenced domestic politics but foreign policy as well. For example, militarists concerned over who the next German enemy might be focused on building the military instead of focusing on international relations. The majority of Germans in all classes generally supported what the military wanted done internationally.[4] One of Bethmann-Hollweg's goals was to bring together the most centrist political parties of the Reichstag— Conservatives, Centre, and National Liberals—to begin defusing the oversized influence of the military, especially in foreign affairs. He proposed a bill but had to abandon this effort as the conservative parties in the Reichstag thought it was too liberal and the National Liberals felt it was not progressive enough.[5]

Relationships with Germany's potential enemies had been declining for a number of years. One of the military's contributions to the souring of foreign relations began at the end of the 19th century. Great Britain was seen as the most powerful possible enemy because of its tremendous navy. The German military pushed to raise the size and power of its navy by increasing the number of battleships and cruisers.[6] As the new chancellor, Bethmann-Hollweg felt that trying to compete with Great Britain's navy had a decimating effect on international relations. He tried to adjust German policies to a more moderate level.[7] An additional problem was a lack of communication and cooperation between the German Foreign Ministry and Kaiser Wilhelm II. For example, in 1905, the kaiser surprised the ministry by inviting the tsar of Russia to meet with him to form a German-Russian alliance. While they agreed on a treaty, the Russian Foreign Ministry concluded it was too restrictive for their country.[8] For Chancellor Bethmann-Hollweg, it was too late to counter the reality already in motion by 1901, the path to an inevitable war. All of Europe was in an arms race.[9] By the time Uncle Richard's family had moved to Cologne, his future as a wartime German soldier was already inevitable.

As Uncle Richard was growing up, political and societal foundations were being established that would have an impact on his adult life. Jewish support for the Social Democratic Party grew tremendously in the latter part of the 19th century because the National Liberal Party, which they had been supporting, had shifted more nationalistic and conservative.[10] For the SDP, human rights were a priority, in particular opposing any kind of antisemitism. Proof was their promotion of Jewish candidates. As a result, even wealthy Jewish capitalists supported the SDP.[11] In the 1912 general election, the Social Democratic Party won 35 percent of the popular vote. That doubled their strength, making them the largest party in the Reichstag.[12] The German-Jewish vote was astounding, as 85 percent voted for the SDP and related left-wing parties.[13]

While the 1912 election must have been exciting as well as inspiring for the majority of German Jews, the new dominance of the Social Democratic Party in the Reichstag ignited fear and opposition from conservative nationalists. Bureaucrats, militarists, soldiers, and monarchists all opposed a democratic republic over a monarchy.[14] What most of the public did not know was that the Kaiser considered the Reichstag "a troop of monkeys and a collection of blockheads and sleepwalkers".[15] Finally, the authoritarian segment of the German political culture revealed that it had contained, for a number of years, a small, but actual Anti-Semite Party. While it was little, it was part of the Reichstag's conservative coalition elected in 1907.[16] The roots for nationalistic, conservative-based antisemitism were already deeply planted when Uncle Richard was a child. While events like the rise of the SDP in the 1912 election might be seen as a decline in antisemitism, underground movements, in fact, intensified anti-Jewish attitudes. While National Socialism would not have succeeded before World War I, there were some prominent conservative groups that occasionally utilized antisemitism for their own purposes.[17] All of this helped to lay a basis for the explosion of German hatred of Jews by the 1930s.

Uncle Richard's childhood focus must have been, like all children, on family, friends, and school. From the time he moved to Cologne in 1907 until the day he graduated on March 19, 1913, Uncle Richard attended the Israel Folk School of Cologne. While this was a Jewish school, it was recognized in 1881 as a city establishment and received financing from the state. It followed the education outline of other German elementary schools but provided the teaching needed for Jewish religious education as well. This included the Hebrew Bible and the Hebrew language necessary for liturgy and history. His final report card lists the school on Schwalbengasse. The school had a new building constructed right after Uncle Richard's time studying there. During World War I, it was used as a military hospital. After the war, it was used as a general hospital, but by 1922, it was once again the Jewish Folk School. In fact, during the 1920s, it became the largest Jewish folk school in Germany. It was liberal and served the majority of Cologne Jewish children during those years.[18] Uncle Richard's summary report card showed his grades almost completely in the upper levels, between "very good" and "good." German history was his highest-graded subject. His knowledge of German history likely influenced many of the cornerstone decisions he made throughout his life in Germany. In the same month as his graduation from elementary school, Uncle Richard also became a certified swimmer.

Clearly, Uncle Richard was planning to follow the general Stern family practice of merchandising. By the time he graduated from the Israel Folk School, his brother Heinrich's business, in which their father had participated, was doing well. The building for the store, which also had their home on the upper floors, was located 33/35 Sterngasse in Cologne and doing well. Uncle Richard took an apprenticeship at Geschwister Wolff, which had business sites in Paris, Brussels, Annaberg, and Plauen, as well as Cologne. He served them from the summer of 1913 until December of 1916. A reference from his supervisor stated, "He has done well. Since April of this year he is an employee in our house. He is busy, reliable and sincere, doing his work thoroughly and with full interest." While doing his apprenticeship, Uncle Richard also took evening classes in marketing. There were lessons he learned that he applied decades later when he worked on businesses in the United States.

There were two sad family events that happened before Uncle Richard reached adulthood. On August 24, 1910, his grandfather, Michael Stern, died. He had lived in the house in Freisheim built by

Seligmann on the property provided for the area's synagogue. Family history was always precious to Uncle Richard. He knew the prominence in the Jewish community the Stern family had in Freisheim/Weilerswist, so this had to be heartbreaking. Likely, it was Uncle Richard who insisted my dad would be given the Hebrew name *Micha'el,* in honor of his grandfather. I knew it was Dad's Hebrew name, as mine is *Ya'akov ben Micha'el* (Jacob son of Michael).

Most upsetting for Uncle Richard had to be the death of his mother, Elise, from lung disease on November 13, 1916. She was already suffering from the disease in 1915, which she shared in a letter to her oldest son, Heinrich. It was likely Elise got it from smoking. Her letters to her children showed the depth of her heart and her studies of Judaism. After helping Thekla settle in Cologne in 1907, she praised her zest for work and quoted an encouragement from a prayer book. Elise assured her daughter that her devotion to hard work would make her boss happy and help her succeed. In writing to Heinrich as a soldier in World War I, she praised him for the depth of his friendships, as she told him what so many of his friends had sent for him.

The Stern family connected with another Jewish family in 1912, the same year as Uncle Richard's bar mitzvah. Henni Stern, the daughter of Markus Stern's brother, Hermann, married Carl Katz. Much like the Stern family, the Katz family was strongly present in Cologne and Essen. There is no question that Uncle Richard felt very close to his first cousin, Henni. Their relationship, continuing with my father's eventual relationship with her sons who made it to London and South Africa in the late 1930s, was deep and caring, all the way up to my father's death in 2008. The Katz family in Cologne was financially impressive, as they had a series of six butcher shops. In the 1920s, some of the butcher shops included a restaurant. As Jews, their huge business success would eventually make them targets of the rising Nazi Party in the late 1920s.

There is little doubt that World War I overturned the entrance of so many German Jews into retail marketing. The war's significance was, of course, far more than a disturbance of the economy. Ultimately, WW I led to a complete remaking of the German government into a modern republic. This caused a split in the outlook of all German citizens between those who preferred a return to an authoritarian government, in their minds a monarchy instead of a republic, and those who supported the republic. Yet, the postwar path would lead to a very different destination.

All of this was connected to the approach Jews felt they must take. Many might have been hesitant about Germany going to war, but the vast majority expressed their patriotism and dedication once the war began in 1914. This was in line with the political party to which so many Jews were tied—the SDP—which actually supported Germany entering the war despite spending years before 1914 trying to lessen the influence of militarists. The vast majority of German Jews also supported a republic to replace a monarchy. The Stern family, including Uncle Richard, shared the same outlook as most German Jews.

The actual entry of Germany into the war on July 28, 1914, created an abnormal unity between all ends of the German political and religious spectrums. Political beliefs were now on hold. Even the bulk of the most liberal and pacifistic German Jews at least began by supporting the war. One possible reason was an emphasis on conflict with Russia, the most despotic and outwardly antisemitic government in Europe.[19] On August 4, 1914, the kaiser gave a speech in which he proclaimed that a person's religion, class, or political affiliation did not matter.[20] No doubt this helped the feeling among the Jews that they would finally experience full equality in Germany. The result was that many upper- and middle-class Jews volunteered for the German army before being officially called to serve.[21]

On August 4, 1914, Uncle Richard's older brother, Heinrich, joined a large group of Jewish army volunteers. He was 25 and served the bulk of his time on the German front lines until the very end of the war. Their father, Markus, served in the military's auxiliary from his mid-to-late-fifties. For most of the first three years of the war, Uncle Richard was in his apprenticeship, then became officially employed at Geschwister Wolff. By the time he entered the German army, there were serious changes in support of the war, as well as growing fear over the possibility of Germany being defeated.

Most of Germany was convinced that there would be a quick victory in the war. The soldiers, heading into their first battles in 1914, would sing German nationalist songs while attacking.[22] Even by the end of 1914, after experiencing a number of bloody battles on the Western Front, the impending destruction of a whole generation of young German men was not yet recognized.[23] In a letter sent by Elisa Stern to her son Heinrich on December 29, 1915, she told him his request for his dad to send oiled, waterproofed boots was declined. She stated that Markus felt no soldier could stand properly on a rampart in an oiled boot, but even more so, she stated the war would probably not last long enough anyway. He was expressing the optimism felt by most Germans, including German Jews.

There are other subjects she discussed that showed the reality of the war by the end of 1915. Their business was doing very poorly, even in the weeks before Christmas, when retailers usually have their best-selling periods. She wrote about the scarcity of food, how it was forbidden for things to be baked, and that it had been two weeks since she was last able to find any butter, eggs, or smoked meat. Yet, she told Heinrich, in positive wording, about the news of his friends and relatives (all Jews), whether they were on leave, having an operation, or where they were placed in the army.

By the middle of 1916, the atmosphere in Germany regarding the war had dramatically changed. The military and conservative political parties did not want the war to end without achieving the annexation of certain territories, the country of Belgium being a primary desire. It was only the Social Democratic Party that insisted the burden of the war could not be tolerated by the German people if the reason for the war was changed from helping an ally (Austria-Hungary) and self-defense to a war of conquest.[24] Reality was that the Allies opposing Germany had the advantage in military technology, plus they were already getting American aid, which provided a huge number of guns and ammunition. In July of

1916, Chancellor Bethmann-Hollweg did not push annexation. He felt peace had to be attempted on the best possible negotiated terms.[25] By August of 1916, even the Kaiser's confidence in Germany's chance for a successful war collapsed. He declared the war was lost, and Germany had to sue for peace.[26]

The decline of the German people's rapture with the war was mirrored within the Jewish community. The largely Jewish-owned liberal press expressed support for a negotiated peace.[27] Eduard Bernstein, a Jewish socialist political leader, asked Jews all over Europe to put pressure on their governments to pursue peace.[28] The kaiser's confidence in German victory collapsed. In addition, despite the kaiser's declaration in 1914 that all religions should be considered equal, hatred of Jews increased as they became the scapegoats of conservative militarist groups for the failure of the German army in the war. Proof of this occurred in October of 1916, when the war minister ordered a "Jew census" in the army to evaluate the number of Jews on the front lines versus the rear.[29] Almost 3,000 Jews had died in battle. More than 7,000 had been decorated. Yet, the war minister fanned the flames of antisemitism by trying to show that Jews were reluctant to serve on the front lines. But this failed, as the census showed that 80 percent served on the front lines.[30] This all developed 11 months before my great uncle entered the army.

On June 20, 1917, Uncle Richard was drafted into the German army, where the atmosphere was very different than when his brother Heinrich volunteered in 1914. Serving as a soldier was not his choice. Much of German society knew they were losing the war. Uncle Richard could not have felt the same enthusiasm as did the early soldiers. But he did feel a sense of obligation to serve his country as best he could to help bring the war to a close with a peace agreement rather than a loss.

His military service booklet from World War I was the equivalent of a soldier's passport. The front showed the symbol of the kaiser. The inside began with the information Germany required other than his basic name and address. His religion was defined as "Israelist." His employment position was listed as a "merchant." The book showed he was not married, had no children, and was from the Prussian state. The officially listed position he served in the infantry was as a musketeer, which was the designation of infantry privates. He was trained in machine-gunning as well as gassing. He was issued a gas mask. The basic rifle assigned to him, as to most German soldiers, was a 98 Carbine. His first army corps was the 36th Infantry Regiment. The service booklet contained a description of how a soldier had to behave and how to get time off. Even after being released from service, they were technically still members of the military, just considered on a leave of absence. This is important to remember in light of a decision the German government would make against Uncle Richard in 1937.

Uncle Richard's basic training ended in August of 1917, and he was briefly sent to join the battle against Russia on the Eastern Front. However, he was clearly being transferred to the Western Front. In a letter by his brother Heinrich to the family at home, Heinrich mentioned that Richard had gone to Brussels to observe Rosh Hashanah and was returning to his regiment that day. In addition, Heinrich reported that Uncle Richard had collected a group of packages containing food and other items Heinrich and his fellow Jewish soldiers could use to celebrate Rosh Hashanah and had them sent to him. Heinrich went to services in Laan, where he saw over 2.000 Jewish soldiers.

By November of 1917, the Bolshevik revolution had successfully placed the Communists in power, and they made it clear that they would withdraw Russia from the war.[31] In November, Uncle Richard began his assignment on the Western Front, where he was transferred into the 2nd Machine Gun Company of the Landwehr Infantry Regiment 31, and fought on the front lines in a series of horrifically violent battles against British and French troops.

In addition to the collapse of Russia's opposition to Germany, there were a number of events during 1917 that gave German militarists a false sense they could successfully push for annexationist peace. A French general was so incompetent that the French army had to deal with mutiny and defeatism. In addition, the Italians suffered a bad defeat in October of 1917.[32] The end of hostilities with Russia gave the German military the ability to transfer a significant number of troops to the Western Front. This enabled the conservative nationalists to gain dominance. Also, this must have created a brief feeling among German soldiers that, finally, the war would shift in their direction, or at least push the Allies to agree to a more beneficial peace agreement for Germany. A postcard dated December 25, 1917, expressing the hope that peace would come shortly, came from Dr. Heinrich Cohn, a rabbi chaplain, who conducted a service where he met Uncle Richard. He assured the Stern family at home in Cologne that he was "healthy and in good spirits." The year 1918 destroyed any German hopes of a beneficial peace.

A statement entered on December 1, 1917, in Uncle Richard's service booklet by the lieutenant commanding his company noted he was a very good gun loader. From the very next day, December 2, he was frequently a soldier in terribly violent battles, a number of which included man-to-man fighting within the trench. On February 21, 1918, he fought as a machine gunner through a tough battle in Flanders, Belgium. Throughout the month of April, Germany launched a spring offensive, and Uncle Richard was often on the front lines. They were consistently in Belgium near Flanders, which was the location of some of the bloodiest battles in World War I. In 1959 Uncle Richard wrote a summary of his life and stated the most difficult frontline battles he experienced were by Flanders, Verdun, and Hartmansweiler. He served as a machine gunner in each battle. By the summer, he was moved to the front line near Alsace-Lorraine, participating in the German offensive near Champagne from July 15 to July 17, once again serving in these battles as a machine gunner.

In summary, Uncle Richard was part of the German offensive counterattack attempts in 1918. There were moments of frightening charges against the Allies' front lines. Each one of them failed, yet he acted with bravery. The casualties from the series of battles he was in were devastating. In the April battle in Flanders alone, 120,000 German soldiers died. The total casualty percentage for the entire German army in WW I was over 54 percent. As a constant frontline soldier, it was very likely that Uncle Richard would die or at least suffer injury. This made his survival almost miraculous. By the end of August, Uncle Richard's unit was in a desperate defense of an Allied counterattack in Lorraine.

In his service booklet, Uncle Richard's behavior was described as being quite good. On August 22, 1918, he was awarded the Iron Cross 2nd Class, which goes to German soldiers who perform at least one act of bravery at a level beyond the requirement of the German army. Still, by the time he received the Iron Cross, it was clear Germany would suffer a devastating defeat. As the war moved into September, the Allied armies of Great Britain, France, and the United States were all pushing forward, devastating the German front lines.[33] By October 12, Uncle Richard's unit had retreated to Beaumont, Belgium. He was there when the war ended on November 11, 1918.

At the end of World War I, Germany not only suffered a military defeat but was also rocked by internal revolution that converted the country from a monarchy to a republic. By the end of September, the most powerful leader of the German army, Gen. Erich Ludendorff, knew defeat was inevitable and told his government they must sue for peace.[34] Ludendorff was one of the nationalistic military conservatives who pushed Russia to give up land to Germany after the Bolsheviks had pulled Russia out of the war. Ludendorff's co-hero to German conservatives was Field Marshal Paul von Hindenburg, who would be the president of the republic when it collapsed in 1933. The actual revolution to end the monarchy for a democratic republic spread throughout the country during the fall of 1918. Many civilians called for this. On October 22, 1918, at a motor construction plant that went on strike, they called for peace and the end of the monarchy, shouting, "The kaiser is a scoundrel!"[35]

These protests spread all over Germany, including to Cologne, the Stern family's hometown.[36] The revolution also reached into segments of the military. There was a navy mutiny on November 5 in which they refused to attack British ships.[37] One of the Social

Democratic Party leaders, Friedrich Ebert, was appointed interim chancellor and given the job of overseeing the transition from a monarchy to a republic.[38] As a couple dozen German states replaced dynasties with republics, numerous German Jews were prominently involved in these regional governments as well as in the new federal government.[39] On November 10, Kaiser Wilhelm II resigned and fled to Holland.[40] Perhaps the most significant development was Ludendorff and other military leaders urging the new republican government to accept the terms of a humiliating armistice. The government did, and the leaders took responsibility for the armistice instead of pushing the responsibility onto the military.[41] That would lay the groundwork for criticism of the Weimar Republic by conservative nationalists for the next 14 years.

As part of the degrading armistice, the victorious Allies gave Germany three days to leave the places they occupied, particularly in Belgium and France, or face renewed hostilities. The handling of soldiers by the German army must have been disorganized, perhaps even panicked, as Uncle Richard's service booklet says he left his regiment on November 27, 1918, without being ordered to do so. Yet, there was no punishment and it says he was assigned to another regiment on December 12. This is a hint that the German army's ability to care for its soldiers was deteriorating. As the army was demobilized, there was a lack of food, clothing, and transportation. On January 16, 1919, it was clear the German government had to get the bulk of its soldiers back to their homes. On that day, Uncle Richard received fifty marks to leave the army, along with six marks for transportation, totaling the equivalent of about twelve dollars. He also received civilian clothing and food coupons that were in effect until February 9.

Uncle Richard not only witnessed historical events during his time in Cologne and service in the German army, but he also became an adult. He celebrated his Bar Mitzvah the same year the political party most supported by the Jews, the SDP, had its most successful election. He saw the regime of Kaiser Wilhelm II, erratic in how it managed international relations as well as its outlook on German Jews. His eldest brother expressed the feelings of many

German Jews at the beginning of the war by volunteering for the army. Heinrich represented the excited feeling of German Jews at the start of World War I through his enthusiastic commitment to Germany's entering the war. Almost three years later, Uncle Richard was drafted at a time when there was little enthusiasm left for the war. He viewed his service as merely necessary to fulfill his obligation as a loyal German citizen. He experienced one of the most awful series of frontline battles of any family member, receiving the Iron Cross, as did a very large portion of the Jewish soldiers. His actions of bravery were not based on a belief that Germany would win the war, but on his patriotism.

Perhaps the most significant occurrences were two tied deeply together: the formation of the Weimar Republic and the strong opposition by conservatives and antisemitic nationalists to that democratic republic replacing the monarchy. No doubt Uncle Richard witnessed the moments in which Jews thought they had achieved true equality in Germany as well as disappointment in the rise of antisemitism. He was one of 100,000 Jews who served in the German army. Twelve thousand were killed in action. Nineteen thousand were promoted to higher ranks, although only 2,000 were officers. Uncle Richard was one of 30,000 Jewish soldiers who received some level of medal for bravery. He viewed his role as a Jew in the German army to be the same as his family forefathers' roles as soldiers from 1812 through 1871. As a liberal German Jew, he saw the negative and positive aspects of the end of the war. Like most Germans, he was sad his country lost. Like most Jews, he endorsed the concept of the Weimar Republic. Uncle Richard must have entered the 1920s as a young man believing that Germany would now practice more of the admirable civic qualities of the United States, the country where he would flee when this dream was destroyed.

Heinrich Stern as a German soldier in 1915

Richard Stern in the German Army, after training (summer of 1917)

Richard Stern in the German Army. just before receiving the Iron Cross (August 15, 1918)

Document of Richard Stern's award of the Iron Cross (August 22, 1918)

---

1. Elon, p 198
2. Ibidem
3. Craig, p 287
4. Idem, p 288
5. Idem, p 289
6. Idem, p 308
7. Idem, p 325
8. Idem, p 321
9. Idem, p 324
10. Elon, p 254

11. Idem, p 255
12. Idem, p 293
13. Idem, p 254
14. Craig, p 293
15. Idem, p 292
16. Idem, p 280
17. Bracher, p. 45
18. Email from Esther Bugaeva from Roonstrasse Synagogue.
19. Elon, p 308
20. Idem, p 309
21. Idem, p 306
22. Craig, p 340
23. Idem, p 344
24. Idem, p 359
25. Idem, p 373
26. Idem, p 374
27. Elon, p 334
28. Idem, p 335
29. Idem, p 338
30. Ibidem
31. Craig, p 389
32. Ibidem
33. Idem, p 395
34. Ibidem
35. Idem, p 397
36. Elon, p 341
37. Ibidem
38. Ibidem
39. Idem, p 343
40. Craig, p 402
41. Elon, p 343

4

THE ROARING TWENTIES (AND NAZIS)

When World War I was over, Uncle Richard made it back to his
family's home in Cologne by the end of February. At that time,
Cologne had the largest Jewish community in all of Germany.
Uncle Richard celebrated his 20th birthday and, just like people all
over America and Germany, he was about to enter the Roaring
Twenties. Just like the worlds of America and Germany, his
personal world had exciting, positive moments, as well as negative
ones that laid the groundwork for some of his future challenges.
Further, he would see the beginning of profound changes that
would take place in the 1930s.

America experienced great industrial and economic growth,
plus a cultural explosion. The 1920s saw the rise of jazz music,
automobiles, radio, telephones, and movies. And women won the
right to vote in 1920. Germany also enjoyed flourishing arts and
sciences. Particularly famous was the Bauhaus movement, which
revolutionized art, architecture, and inspired modern design in a
wide range of products. With the establishment of the Weimar
Republic, women got the right to vote in 1919, even before
American women. For German Jews, the Roaring Twenties
included full legal equality; university professorships finally
opened up to Jews. Without question, for the German-Jewish

community as well as millions of German liberals and Social Democrats, the most positive "roar" was the development of the Weimar Republic, which created hope and a fresh start for Germany.[1]

Yet, there was negative "roaring" in both the United States and Germany. The United States placed strict limits on immigration, which would have a devastating impact on German Jews in the 1930s. The negative roaring in Germany was more complex than in America. Being the defeated country in World War I created a range of difficulty and hated situations in Germany during the 1920s. French and British troops occupied western parts of Germany. Cologne housed British troops. The Allies required Germany to pay massive reparations beginning in August of 1919 and rising to twenty billion gold marks by May of 1920.[2] The result would be economic setbacks, compared to the constant economic growth during the 1920s in America. These aspects of the Versailles Treaty cultivated serious opposition to the very existence of a democratic republic. While initial opposition came from the same conservative, militarist, pro-monarchy political parties, the most significant development was the rise of the Nazi Party. All of this reinflamed Germany's temporarily dormant antisemitism.

Uncle Richard's personal "Roaring Twenties" began with great hope. He had not just survived the war; he had been decorated with an Iron Cross and was a respected German-Jewish war veteran. He felt lucky to be living in Cologne, where the Jewish community appreciated Mayor Adenauer's behavior. Cologne had 16,000 Jews, about 2.3 percent of the city's whole population. My uncle believed he had the opportunity to be a successful merchant. He believed in the new government, the Weimar Republic. Yet his hopes would be dashed by heartbreaking family events, some strictly personal and some caused by the more-violent revival in anti-Jewish hatred.

Just as 1922 and 1923 were eventful years in all of Germany, key events occurred in the Stern family. Richard could not have

43

predicted how these years would twist his life's path. As an active young man starting his 20s, he imagined he would earn good money in business and have plenty of fun with friends and family. There was so much in Cologne he loved. In some ways, it was a liberal city with a large Jewish community. Along with pretty much everyone in Cologne, he had a fabulous time during the yearly *Karneval*. His adult life began with a sense of living in prosperity, good personal relationships, and fun.

In September of 1920, Uncle Richard started his first postwar job as a commercial employee for his uncle, Leopold Stern, who owned a wholesale fabric and textile store in Cologne at 18 Glockengasse. Leopold was a younger brother of Markus Stern. Leopold had married Frieda Billigheimer from Wurzburg in southern Germany in 1891. They had one daughter, Irene, born in 1899. He was quite financially successful, as he owned two homes, one on Pionierstasse and the other on Mainzer Strasse. Leopold and his wife lived in a stately home with six elaborately decorated rooms. Their daughter Irene got married in the early 1920s, had a daughter in 1928, got divorced shortly afterward, and immigrated to the United States in 1934.

Uncle Richard's father, Markus, worked in Heinrich's store and lived with his son in the Sterngasse home. During the war, Markus individually managed the store as Heinrich served in the German army. Its sales suffered tremendously during the war. By 1922, Markus realized he needed a new location to live and work, as Heinrich married Frieda Lowy in March of 1923. At some point in 1922, Markus obtained 20 Marsilstein. Like many of the buildings in that area of Cologne, the ground floor was a business, and the upper floors the family's home. Markus Stern opened a new bedding store on the ground floor. Upstairs were the living quarters. The second floor contained the kitchen, dining room, library, and bathroom. On the third floor were three bedrooms. Extra rooms were on the fourth floor. Use of these rooms would change dramatically from the 1920s to the late 1930s.

Because Markus struggled financially during the war, he needed help from his brother Leopold to acquire the building and create the store. The name of the business was House Stern's Special Bedding. Leopold lent him five thousand marks. By late 1923, the new bedding store was open. Markus then asked Uncle Richard to join the new business. At 62 years old, Markus wanted to make sure a young family member would run the bedding store. With solid investments in other real estate, Leopold decided to close his wholesale textile store, where Richard had worked. It was closed by 1925. Leopold was listed in Cologne's archives as connected to the new Stern bedding store, an additional investment.

Those years of 1922 and 1923 contained another significant Stern family story, the relationship between my nana Martha Stern and Walter Romberg. One of 13 siblings, Walter was born in Diepholtz, Germany, on February 26, 1893, and had moved to Cologne by the time he was 20. Walter Romberg was a soldier during World War I, and he told stories about the war like it was a fun adventure. His daughter from his second marriage in 1932 did not understand how he could have liked the war because he was a communist, active in the KPD, the German communist party. Walter was not at all religious and pretty much avoided going to a synagogue. He had a hard time succeeding in any kind of work or business, moving from job to job—from a buyer for a company to a traveling farm machinery salesman.

In fact, Walter Romberg's siblings considered him to be the black sheep of their family. His ambivalence toward Judaism stood in contrast to many of his siblings and particularly his father, Julius Romberg, and his grandfather, Nathan Romberg. Walter's grandfather Nathan was among the Jewish leaders who created the synagogue in Lengerich during the 1840s, purchasing a Torah that he lent for use in the synagogue. Julius Romberg helped build the Jewish congregation in Diepholz by donating that Torah. He brought it to Diepholz in 1865. The congregation in Lengerich actually sued Julius for taking the Torah scroll, claiming it belonged to them. The court, however, ruled that the Romberg family owned it, so Julius, as the main inheritor, could take it where he wanted.

A number of his siblings also served in the German army in a much more notable way than Walter. One brother, Alfred, was the family's hero because he was among the first Jewish commissioned officers in the German army in World War I, winning an Iron Cross. His siblings were not communists, and most supported the Social Democratic Party. Most were also much more successful in business. One of his older brothers, Siegfried, owned an upper-end men's clothing store and a tie factory. The very youngest brother, Karl, ran an extremely successful wool importing business in partnership with some Englishmen. Karl's son Ralph remembered how Walter would come from Cologne to visit Karl in Essen to get financial aid from him, but he would also bring candy treats to Karl's two sons and share his dark humor.

Walter Romberg had an affair with a woman that resulted in a baby boy. Despite this, he clearly appealed enough to Martha Stern to have an affair with Walter at some point in the latter half of 1922. They were forced to get married on March 9, 1923, before Martha gave birth to her son Rudi, my dad, on July 11, 1923. They moved into an apartment to live together at 28 Ulrichgasse in Cologne. However, by the end of 1924, Walter left Martha. Most of the Stern family would condemn Walter for the rest of their lives. Yet, the relationship was very complicated. All broken relationships are caused by complications by both partners. Walter and his family referred to Martha as "the red-haired beast" because of her sharp, explosive temper observed by many people throughout her life. My uncle never had anything good to say about Walter Romberg. He despised the way Walter treated his sister, to whom he was protective until the end of her life. He probably disliked Walter's uncaring attitude toward Judaism and could not stand Walter's communist beliefs.

Martha took a job as a cashier in one of the Katz family's butcher shops to earn an income. By the beginning of 1925, Martha, with her one-and-a-half-year-old son, moved into her father, Markus's, house on 20 Marsilstein. Uncle Richard was already living there. Even though there were plenty of bedrooms, he shared one with young Rudi. Their deep relationship was underway by the time Rudi turned two in 1925.

Like the Stern family, there were happy and sad things occurring in Germany from 1922 to 1925. The Versailles Treaty, signed by the Weimar Republic government in June of 1919, caused tremendous backlash to this new style of government by political parties representing conservative nationalists, militarists, and monarchists. Even though these parties participated in Reichstag elections during the 1920s, they followed a philosophy that created these tendencies: anti-intellectualism, acceptance of violence, and political indifference. These reflected an attitude that honorableness was less important than obedience.[3] The conservative parties believed their positions were justified by the Versailles Treaty's requirement to pay reparations to the Allies and the Allied occupation of parts of western Germany.

Inflation was rampant in Germany during and after the war. Postwar reparations to the victorious Allies caused massive inflation in the early 1920s.[4] In 1914, there were 4.2 marks to the dollar. Just after Versailles in 1919, it had risen to fourteen marks to the dollar. By mid-1920, it was 39.5 marks to the dollar. After inflation exploded, it rose to 4.2 trillion marks to the dollar by November of 1923,[5] Inflation hit business owners harder than the war.[6] The war was started by conservatives, but the inflation was blamed on the liberals who formed the republic. High prices also likely contributed to Markus Stern leaving Heinrich's business and his need to have his more financially sound brother Leopold help him create the new store. By the end of 1924, when the new Stern business was operating with Richard's involvement, inflation had dropped to a much more normal range.

Another problem for the Weimar Republic from its earliest days was violence. An iconic episode was the assassination of Walther Rathenau, who had been a successful leader of a segment of the War Department in 1914. Earlier in his life, Rathenau was a monarchist but became a supporter of the Weimar Republic. He first served as the minister of reconstruction, and by February of 1922, became Germany's foreign minister.[7] Rathenau tried hard to improve the relationship between Germany and the nations who defeated it by strictly following the Versailles Treaty. This enraged the monarchist, militarist, and conservative nationalist parties.[8] Rathenau was Jewish, which further infuriated ultra-right-wing groups. There were violent protests against him outside the Reichstag with rioters screaming, "Kill off Walther Rathenau, the greedy goddamn Jewish sow!" On June 24, he was assassinated, becoming the 354th political assassination by right-wing nationalists.[9] Rathenau's murder was more than a political action. It was an expression of antisemitism embraced by a new party, the National Socialist Workers' Party—the Nazis.

Nazism is very often only connected to the leadership success of Adolf Hitler. However, when he took power in 1933, a bulk of Germany overwhelmingly accepted his radical antisemitism. Because of his propaganda of German nationalist superiority, his support for the military, and the Nazi Party's claim that represented the average worker, his dictatorship was accepted in lieu of the desire to return to monarchy. Germany already had a strain of nationalism that opposed aliens, setting a path for Hitler's success.[10] A group of nationalistic monarchists attempted to overthrow the Weimar Republic in March of 1920. Ultra-right-wing parties that opposed the concept of a democratic republic formed immediately after the war ended. In 1919, Hitler joined a German worker's party in Munich.[11] This was an ultra-right nationalistic party that claimed to represent the interest of German workers as opposed to communism. It evolved into the National Socialist Worker's party by 1921, and a party meeting on July 29, 1921, had 550 members.[12] Around that time, Hitler was able to take over the party's main leadership and formed its paramilitary, the SA, into an instrument of "fear and terror."[13] This created a militaristic air for the party, laying the groundwork for support from those who loved the military as well as nationalism. From early on, Jews were forbidden from joining the party.

Even in the early '20s, the Nazi Party grew significantly. At the beginning of 1922, it had 6,000 members. By September of 1923, it had grown to 55,000 members.[14] On November 8-9 of 1923, Hitler and his Nazis violently attempted to take control of the government in Munich. What became known as the Beer Hall Putsch failed, and in February 1924, Hitler and other Nazi Party leaders were tried in court. He did not claim innocence. Instead, he used his testimony to justify his attempted coup, pointing out the problems of the Versailles Treaty and the nationalists' perspectives on the difficulties Germans were suffering under the republic. There were men in the court who agreed with Hitler's position.[15] He was put in prison for only nine months.

In the elections of May 1924, serious developments hinted at an eventual failure of the Weimar Republic. First, the Communist Party gained almost as many seats in the Reichstag as the Center Party, which was one of the parties in the governing coalition.[16] In addition, radical right-wing antisemitic parties began taking part in elections instead of just violently protesting. Hitler was not yet an official German citizen, so he could not take any government seat. Instead, he published *Mein Kampf* in July of 1925. Hitler not only attracted antisemites, his opposition to civil order, moral values, and the structure of the Weimar Republic resonated with those in the poorest classes and among young people.[17]

By 1928 the Nazi Party had grown to a hundred thousand strong, with a huge number of members under 30. It referred to the Weimar Republic as the "Jew Republic." Yet, in 1928, because of the relative economic stability and a trend toward peace in Germany after 1924, the Social Democratic Party regained their Reichstag strength in the elections. The leader of the SDP, Hermann Muller, became Germany's chancellor. A coalition of the SDP, another moderate left-wing party, and the Center Party was formed to lead the Reichstag. The ultra-right-wing parties lost a chunk of their seats in the Reichstag.[18] This made the eventual result from the elections of 1932, and Hitler's rise to the chancellorship in 1933, unpredictable to left-wing Germans and German Jews. That included the Stern family.

For Uncle Richard, 1928 brought a major change to his life. By the middle of 1927, his father, Markus, was deeply ill. The family knew he could not live much longer. On December 28, Markus

Stern transferred ownership of his share of the bedding store to Uncle Richard. The document was handwritten by Markus and stated that his son would be the business's sole owner, then it was signed by him and Uncle Richard. As the executor, my uncle was required to divide three thousand marks, interest free, among the rest of the Stern family listed in his father's will within one year after Markus's death. Ownership of the living quarters was also transferred to Richard. Finally, there was an agreement to continue the repayment of a 5,000-mark loan to Leopold Stern. On January 23, 1928, Markus Stern died. Just a few days before Markus's death, my uncle pledged to take care of his sister Martha and her son Rudi, my dad, and never abandon them. That is when he became Rudi's legal guardian.

Despite the mourning over Markus's death, the beginning of 1928 started four years of an enjoyable life for Uncle Richard and his nephew, my dad. The bedding business hit its greatest period of success, earning Uncle Richard as much as fifty thousand marks per year. This amount was enough to hire domestic help that lived on the very top floor of 20 Marsilstein. In the adjoining house, 18 Marsilstein, lived Uncle Richard's sister Thekla, her husband, Heinz, and their two daughters, Ruth and Ellen. Thekla's marriage was interfaith, as Heinz Flogerhover was a nonpracticing Catholic. He owned a print shop. Dad loved living next door to his cousins. In fact, he was only a few minutes' walk from all of his cousins as well as his very close friend Lothar Gruenbaum. He could easily play with the children he loved as a little boy.

While Thekla's intermarriage was the only one among the Stern siblings, it was not unusual for German Jews in the 1920s. Mixed marriages were at an all-time high, only equaled 50 years later in the United States.[19] A large segment of the Cologne Jewish community was so assimilated into German Christian society, many had no interest in connecting to Jewish institutions. Many of their children attended Catholic or Protestant elementary schools.[20] Although the Stern family was not Orthodox in their Jewish observance, they were deeply connected to the Jewish community. Dad began attending the Israel Folk School, the same elementary school as Uncle Richard, in 1929. His cousins, Aunt Thekla's daughters, also attended the school.

He continued the family's membership in the Roonstrasse Synagogue, although he did not attend Shabbat services every week. My uncle always observed the High Holidays, when a ticket was required for attendance. The level of their donations decided every congregant's seat assignments. Once at the service, they could not leave during the Torah reading or the sermon. Children under six years old were not allowed to be at the High Holiday services, and communications of any kind were forbidden during services. Uncle Richard arranged for Rudi to attend the Glockengasse Synagogue, a more conservative one, where he became part of an all-male choir. Rudi sang as a soprano in the choir and attended Shabbat services almost every week as a young boy.

Treating my dad as his son was one of the centerpieces of Uncle Richard's life. He took his nephew for an outing every Sunday. Most often, it was a hike. While walking home, they would stop at a café for a fresh-baked treat or some ice cream. As an adult, my dad spoke about how he watched Uncle Richard treat everybody honorably, whether as a businessman, a family member, or a friend. Throughout his childhood, Dad noticed how my uncle was always the humorous centerpiece of a party with friends and family. During these years in the 1920s, Uncle Richard became Chanukah Man for a group of Stern family children.

Uncle Richard was an active Social Democrat. He tried to raise his nephew with the same liberal values. Like much of the Jewish community, he strongly supported the Weimar Republic, even when there were obvious problems within the government. Having studied German history, he felt the Republic protected people's freedoms more completely than any prior German government. He would often take Dad to political demonstrations as well as political party meetings. Dad would sit through long political speeches, which bored him as a young child. One of the most significant outings he had with Uncle Richard was on June 30, 1930. Uncle Richard lifted him onto his shoulders and carried him to the square outside the major Catholic Cathedral of Cologne. They celebrated the departure of the last British troops who had occupied the Rhineland. His nephew was being trained to support the democratic republic and be a patriotic German, exactly as Uncle Richard grew up.

Perhaps the most fun he had during those years was taking part in the Cologne *Karneval* every year, usually in February. *Karneval* (very similar to the New Orleans Mardi Gras) is at the end of a period of time called *Fasching*, which begins on November 11, closing before Ash Wednesday of the Catholic Church. It is a celebration about breaking the normal rules and creating funny versions of your own. Typical participation in *Karneval* activities involves dressing in costumes, including masks. Many of the *Karneval* marches in Cologne went right by the Stern residence on Marsilstein. In general, Uncle Richard loved standing in his store's doorway to greet friends, family, and customers. Even more fun was participating in the *Karneval* by standing in the doorway during all of the celebrations going down his street. He dressed in crazy costumes and joined in many of the activities. He often had fun with relatives and potential girlfriends, leading groups of friends and family in their *Karneval* enjoyment. There is a photo of Uncle Richard with two women in costumes, Hedy Juda, who he liked to hang out with, and Grete Lind, his cousin.

During the bulk of the 1920s, Uncle Richard lived a life that combined his German patriotism, political support for the Weimar Republic, dedication to the Jewish people, the love of raising his nephew, and having fun with family and friends and girlfriends. He was admired for his combination of seriousness when necessary and humor whenever appropriate. As the 1930s approached, he felt his life was on an upward path. There were, unfortunately, events that gave hints about what was actually going to happen next.

One time in first grade, I sang a racist song to myself that included the N-word. I had heard it from a classmate. It was to the tune of "Jingle Bells." Someone working at our home heard me singing and told my parents. On Sunday mornings, before getting dressed to go to Sunday school at our temple, I would go into my parents' bedroom and play with Dad. That Sunday, when I entered their bedroom, Dad told me to sit down. I could see he was upset with me, his temples red and pulsing. I had no idea why. He told me he heard about what I had sung, that it was a horrible insult to black people, and I should never, ever use those words again. Then, for the first time, he told me about some of his experiences as a Jew in Germany, that there were Germans who mocked Jews and called them names. Dad stressed how the name-calling was so horrible, it spoiled the lives of German Jews. He made it clear that I should never use words that could ruin any person's life. Dad saw the treatment of African Americans in the context of what he experienced in Germany. That moment in my childhood, even at just six years old, opened my mind to the importance of civil rights and to never disrespect a person because of their ethnicity.

In the late 1920s, while still a minor movement, the Nazi Party had grown enough in popularity to put on some public demonstrations. Nazis would stage a march down the streets, singing songs mocking the Jews. Dad recalled the Nazis saying they would throw flowers as Germany got rid of its Jews. Uncle Richard repeated the response of left-wing politicians, "Don't forget to throw the flower pots at the Nazis." While Uncle Richard, Martha, and Dad did not personally experience an attack by Nazis in the late 1920s, their relatives in the Katz family, who employed Martha, had an awful confrontation.

The Katz family was partners with the Rosenthal family in a hugely successful chain of butcher shops throughout Cologne. In 1928, the Katz-Rosenthal-owned company rose to a high point of commercial success with six butcher shop locations throughout western Cologne. In February of 1928, they added to their business by opening an American-style self-service restaurant. Rosa Katz Rosenthal was a family member playing a key management role in the restaurant. A customer would pay, get a receipt, and receive their food at the pickup counter. There were no other restaurants similar to this in Cologne.

The Nazi Party in Cologne published a weekly propaganda magazine called *Westdeutscher Beobachter*, the *West German Observer*. They printed an article that claimed this new Katz-Rosenthal snack bar, as it was connected to the butcher shop chain, would spread around Cologne in a way that would cause other butcher shops to close. The accusation by the Nazi magazine created ugly anger against the Katz-Rosenthal business, among other butchery owners. That laid the root for a staged, nasty personal incident. On April 14, 1928, an amateur boxer named Jakob Domgörgen and his friend Karl Wower came to the restaurant and ordered goulash. The boxer complained to the kitchen manager about the food. Rosa arrived, and it was inspected. An argument broke out, getting a little physical. It ended with a stain on the boxer's suit. The boxer claimed there was a dead mouse found in the goulash. The woman in charge of the kitchen said that was not possible and even kept the goulash around for a couple of days to be inspected before throwing it out.

Rosa reported the two men to the police, claiming they were trying to blackmail the owners. In response, Domgörgen filed a case against the Katz-Rosenthal business, claiming the incident prevented him from being physically able to participate in any boxing. On April 22, the two parties met, and each agreed to withdraw their complaints. Two weeks later, *Westdeutscher Beobachter* ran an article using antisemitic slander to make a claim of unsanitary conditions in the restaurant. A month later, it published a more detailed article, claiming the boxer found a fried dead mouse and saying the Katz-Rosenthal business, typical of Jews, was cheating in its attempt to hide their misconduct. At one point, a Social Democratic newspaper published an article condemning the Nazi magazine's article as "fodder" to justify antisemitic campaign propaganda. At a public Nazi meeting on June 5, this was stated: "The Jew is the biggest criminal that history has ever known. And the Jewish butchers have conglomerated with the single aim of poisoning each and every Christian alive today."[21]

The accusations by the Nazi Party in Cologne against the Katz-Rosenthal business seemed unending. *Westdeutscher Beobachter* kept running articles attacking the Jewish business, each one leveling false claims such as bribery. The Nazi Party claimed their paper represented the true interests of the German nation. By 1929, the whole affair had been investigated, and was there was a court trial. The Nazi magazine was told to stop publishing articles about this incident. The legal accusations against the Katz-Rosenthal business were dropped as the investigation concluded that the claim of the mouse in the goulash was false. The Katz-Rosenthal business sued the Nazi magazine, claiming that its purpose was solely antisemitism. The court did not rule in their favor, as they saw the first article not as specifically antisemitic but an attempt to have an investigation into the accusation of poisoned food carried out. The court did not acknowledge the articles by *Westdeutcher Beobachter* simply as antisemitic propaganda. In two books published by the Nazis during the Third Reich, this incident was called "Katz-Rosenthal and the Mouse."[22] This is a small part of the many details of this incident, and the antisemitic suffering of the Katz family was researched by Michael Vieten, who wrote about the Katz family's history.

The failure of the Cologne court to give any protection against anti-Jewish slander was typical of German courts by this time in the 1920s. German Jews were supportive of the Weimar Republic, but the undermining of it by the conservative political parties was underway through the court system.[23] The disappointing ruling by the Cologne court was a demonstration of how wrong the common Jewish feeling was about Cologne being safer for them than the rest of Germany. They had no clue how this accusation of the Katz-Rosenthal business would return in 1933.

My uncle entered the 1930s as a successful merchant. He was typical of the Jewish middle/upper-middle class, combining patriotism, political involvement in a liberal party, and support of the post-World War I government. He had the responsibility of taking care of his sister Martha and raising her son, my dad Rudi. He most likely thought at some point in the near future he would find his own lifelong partner. Like most Jews in Cologne, he did not suspect that incidents such as the one suffered by his relatives in the Katz family would become the roots for an unstoppable change in his life's path. The Sterns and the Katz family were very assimilated into Germany, with many non-Jewish friends. Even though antisemitism had always been part of German history, there was no expectation it would become a key basis for the establishment of a German dictatorship.

Martha (née Stern) Romberg with her son Rudi (1928)

Hedy Juda, Richard Stern, Grete Lind dressed up for Karneval (1930)

---

1. Elon, p 358
2. Craig, p 437
3. Idem, p 491

4. Idem, p 441
5. Idem, p 450
6. Idem, p 453
7. Idem, p 441
8. Elon, p 363
9. Idem, p 370
10. Bracher, p 63
11. Idem, p 79
12. Idem, p 92
13. Idem, p 88
14. Idem, p 100
15. Idem, p 119
16. Idem, p 123
17. Idem, p 128
18. Idem, p 125
19. Elon, p 377
20. Cologne During National Socialism, p 183
21. Vieten, p 96
22. Idem, p 106
23. Elon, p 374

5

THE DOORWAY

During all the years I would visit Uncle Richard, I noticed he often had an American flag hanging on the front of his house. After we moved to Allentown, I saw the flag displayed for any possible American holiday or celebration. After learning he had served in the US Army, I figured Uncle Richard was simply expressing his patriotism to the United States. Years later, when I studied the history of the Nazi Party's rise to power in the early 1930s, I began to understand a potentially deeper reason.

As the Nazi Party surged in popularity during the early 1930s, Uncle Richard and my dad noticed two developments. One was a huge increase in Nazi marches that turned more vocal and more violent. The other was the rising number of houses displaying swastika flags, especially after Hitler was appointed the chancellor on January 30, 1933. The swastika flag symbolized the beginning of intense Jewish oppression and the end of the Weimar Republic. The sight of so many Nazi flags was emotionally devastating for the family, creating fear and anger.

My uncle's constant display of the American flag symbolized the civic, moral American values lacking in Nazi Germany, the values he saw die when the Weimar Republic died. In addition to protesting Jewish oppression by Hitler, he believed he needed to

58

represent civil rights. It was on April 1, 1933, that he transitioned from a fun, successful German-Jewish citizen to a man of moral courage.

Following their poor showing in the 1928 elections, Hitler led the Nazi Party's rise, beginning with speeches and propaganda against the Weimar Republic's foreign policy. He stressed the importance of German nationalism over faith in world peace. His main point was that increasing Germany's nationalistic strength was the most important approach.[1] Like other right-wing parties, this included deriding the Weimar Republic as a source of weakness and the need to rebuild the military. What accelerated Hitler and the Nazi Party's success was the stock market crash on October 24, 1929—Black Friday in the United States. The effects on Germany were numerous, including loss of loans from American banks used to pay off the reparations required by the Versailles Treaty. Psychologically, it revived the memories of the economic disaster caused by the extreme inflation of the early 1920s.[2] From 1930 to 1933, unemployment kept rising dramatically. All of these developments provided the basis for the increasingly popular Nazi propaganda against the Weimar Republic.

Extreme job losses for the working class made people flock toward radical political parties: the Communist Party on the left and the Nazi Party on the right. The United States was experiencing an economic depression as much as Germany, but many groups in Germany saw the Great Depression as a failure of the democratic republic political system.[3] This laid the groundwork for the success of radical authoritarianism, specifically the Nazi Party, which was unintentionally aided by the German president, Paul von Hindenburg.

In the Weimar Republic, the president was elected separately from the Reichstag and had a range of executive powers. Hindenburg was a leading field marshal of the German Army during World War I. His focus was always on maintaining the strength and priorities of the military. Hindenburg was elected president by a narrow margin in 1925. His election was seen by many to have a negative impact on German democracy;[4] however, during his first five years in office, he did not give in to the arguments of his nationalist friends but worked with the political parties in using his authority to address dilemmas.[5]

As the economic crises continued from the end of 1929 into the spring of 1930, Chancellor Hermann Muller asked Hindenburg to grant him emergency powers. Muller had been elected as the chancellor in 1928 and was the last SDP member to serve in that role.[6] Hindenburg refused, so Muller and his cabinet resigned in March of 1930.[7] Hindenburg then appointed a presidential cabinet to administer the government without consulting the Reichstag. He appointed Heinrich Bruning of the Centre Party as chancellor because his positions were more moderate but well respected.[8] In July of 1930, the Reichstag refused to approve Hindenburg's use of emergency power for these appointments, so Bruning dissolved the cabinet and set an election for September 1930. The Reichstag was a parliament with 577 seats filled by multiple parties. For many in established politics, the result was shocking. The Nazi Party became the second-largest party in the Reichstag, rising from 12 to 107 members. By the end of 1930, Bruning was appointed as Germany's official chancellor. The crisis in Germany continued to deepen.

The biggest result for Hitler and the Nazi Party from the 1930 election was his full establishment as a politician, either greatly feared or greatly admired. He was a master of political propaganda. In his book, *Mein Kampf*, which he wrote mostly during his prison term, he declared how propaganda had to be popular and achieved by focusing on the lowest intellect level of the masses. He described most of the population as having low intelligence and how they tended to forget most facts or historical events. Hitler said that people can only handle small falsehoods and could not believe anyone could create a tremendous lie. He presented his own version of "facts" in speeches by never providing qualifications or conceding any issue to an opponent. His propaganda was based on this concept: the bigger the lie, the more likely it would be believed. In addition, his political campaigns included vicious, untrue attacks against the character and reputation of his opponents.[9] He ran print media that disguised propaganda as actual news. An example in Cologne was *Westdeutcher Beobachter*, the paper that wrote against the Katz family in 1928-29.

Although the Nazi Party was known as the National Socialist German Workers' Party (NSDAP), which appealed to some of the working class, Hitler's approach had nothing to do with the general population's needs. He saw his revolutionary goal as not meant for the people but an elite, racially superior leadership. The Nazis would call the Weimar Republic the "Jew Republic." Their success in oppressing and getting rid of the Jews and others they considered racially inferior was the centerpiece of Hitler's ideology.[10] All of these approaches laid the basis for his refusal to accept any offer, result, or situation that was a compromise between his Nazi Party and anyone else.

In September 1931, Jewish storefronts in Berlin were smashed in an eruption of Nazi-originated street violence. A group of Nazi hoodlums attacked a group of Jews leaving their synagogue on Rosh Hashanah.[11] Despite this type of violence, in addition to Hitler and the Nazi Party's campaign approach, no one was ready to believe how Hitler would end up in power within a short time. Hitler knew that brutality attracted as many people as it sickened.[12]

The popularity of the Nazi Party convinced Hindenburg that it should be part of a coalition necessary to avoid another election. Hindenburg pushed Chancellor Bruning to recruit Hitler and the Nazis. Bruning failed. In the spring of 1932, Bruning was dismissed by Hindenburg. Franz von Papen was installed, without any vote by the Reichstag, as the chancellor. Papen was a conservative many considered to be incompetent, but he had many contacts and connections. The idea was to form a wide-range coalition government, and Hitler was invited to become part of it, but not as chancellor. He refused. The violent public conflicts between Nazis and their opponents multiplied over the first several weeks of the summer of 1932. Nazi parades led to battles that killed numerous people.

On July 31, 1932, there was an election that saw the Nazi Party became the largest in the Reichstag, increasing from 107 to 230 seats out of a total of 577. Papen offered Hitler the vice chancellorship. Again, he refused. The election also saw a rise in support for the Communist Party, becoming the third-largest in the Reichstag. Papen and Hindenburg failed in getting Hitler to become part of a coalition government by the fall of 1932. Another Reichstag election was held in November. The Nazi Party lost 34 seats and the Communist Party, while still the third-largest party, gained 11 to rise to 100 seats. The gains of the Communist Party frightened conservatives. Hindenburg and his fellow conservatives, who had desired a return to monarchy, were more worried about communism than preserving the democratic Weimar Republic.

Hindenburg had the power to decide who would become the chancellor. For years he had been approaching decisions as an authoritarian. Hindenburg wanted his favorite person, Papen, to be the chancellor of a coalition government, preventing the rise of the Communist Party's power, of which the Nazi Party would be a member. Papen, however, realized Hitler would only agree if he were given the chancellorship. He began secret meetings with Hitler in the home of a Cologne banker on January 4, 1933.[13] By January 30, 1933, an agreement was reached between Papen, Hindenburg, and Hitler for Hitler to take the chancellorship. Hindenburg was mistakenly convinced that taking on responsibility in a multiparty cabinet would keep Hitler under control. There were a small number of conservative, wealthy Jews who agreed with this.[14]

By January 31, 1933, the Stern family, along with all the Jews in Cologne, saw a shocking number of Nazi flags hanging from stores and houses all over the city. It was a celebration of Hitler's rise to the chancellorship. Most Jews thought this would be temporary.

Once Hitler became chancellor, the Nazi Party, instead of being a party on the decline, became a party gaining advantage from the worldwide economic recovery. This paralleled Hitler's and the Nazis' push to overturn the republican government, not to a president-centered authoritarian rule, but to a single-party totalitarian dictatorship. On February 1, 1933, Hitler convinced Hindenburg to dissolve the Reichstag once again, setting an election for March 5. Hitler got some emergency authority and was able to greatly limit the freedom of the press and expressions of other political opinions.[15] On February 27, the Reichstag building burned down. While never proven, there is suspicion it was arranged by the Nazi Party. On February 28, Hitler was officially given emergency dictatorial powers, which he used to persecute and arrest members of the left-wing parties such as the Social Democratic Party. Despite all of these actions, the Nazi Party did not win a majority of votes (43.9 percent). The left-wing parties still received over 30 percent. On March 23, 1933, the Reichstag passed the Enabling Act, which awarded Hitler "legal" dictatorial powers.[16]

On February 17, 1933, Hitler ordered all local police headquarters to create working relationships with the Nazi Party's SA and SS.[17] All of these rapid developments in the first few months of 1933 set the stage for the beginning of Hitler's officially organized suppression of Germany's Jews. Unofficial attacks against the Jewish community had already started. On March 8, some of the Roonstrasse Synagogue's windows were smashed. A few days later, some members of the SA went into Cologne's kosher slaughterhouse, forced out the Jewish religious officials, then compelled the Jewish merchants to make monetary "donations" to the Nazi Party.[18] There were similar anti-Jewish actions occurring all over Germany, and foreign newspapers were reporting on some of them, creating a potentially negative view of the new Hitler/Nazi Party government within its first few months of existence. Jewish organizations were worried about these activities, but there was no agreement between various Jewish leaders over how this should be approached. The Nazi government, however, blamed the negative reports in the foreign press on Jews.

A Nazi Party executive put together a detailed plan for the first nationally organized action against German Jews. It called for an official boycott of Jewish businesses, Jewish merchandise, Jewish doctors, and Jewish lawyers for April 1, 1933.

"The organizing committees are responsible for making the boycott impact no innocents but the guilty all the harder," the plan stated. To make clear who was "guilty," the plan continued, "The boycott is a purely defensive measure directed exclusively against German Jews."

The organizing committees were told that the boycott had to be carried out by all the German people and affect the Jews "in their most sensitive place." There were instructions for propaganda and "education" to all Germans to cease purchasing from Jewish businesses. The plan called for a sudden, not a gradual, start of the boycott. It ordered the SA and SS to set up warnings to people not to enter Jewish stores.

It was clear from the boycott plan that the Nazis intended to control news organizations. It stated:

> "The action committees closely monitor the newspapers to what extent they participate in the German people's clarification struggle against the Jewish atrocity campaign abroad. If newspapers do not do this or do too little, they must immediately be removed from every house where Germans live. No German and no German business should advertise in such newspapers. They must fall to public contempt, written for members of the Jewish race but not for the German people."[19]

The organizers of the boycott were commanded to make sure any German citizen with foreign connections "spread the truth that calm and order reign in Germany, that the German people have no more intense desire than to do its work in peace and to live in peace with the outside world, and that it only wages the struggle against the Jewish atrocity campaign as a purely defensive struggle." In addition, advertisements were placed in newspapers announcing the boycott.

Although the official boycott was to begin "suddenly, not gradually," boycotts of Jewish businesses had already been underway by the middle of March 1933. The Jewish community knew a large, officially organized boycott was about to happen on April 1, 1933. There was panic, along with arguments over how to respond to the antisemitic actions by the Nazi government. The president of the Cologne Synagogue Community published a statement, co-signed by the rabbinate, demonstrating to the Nazi government the Jewish community's dedication to German patriotism despite the negative foreign newspaper reports about what was unfolding in Germany. In the *Newsletter of the Cologne Synagogue Community,* they stated, "We are most deeply convinced that German Jews in their historic and innate attachment to the German people are willing and determined to participate in the buildup and rise of the fatherland. We have today arranged for distribution abroad of this declaration."[20] This expression of Jewish patriotism, meant to pacify Nazi actions against the Jews, failed completely.

It had been five years since the Cologne Nazi magazine *Westdeutscher Beobachter* had published continuous anti-Jewish slander articles against the Katz-Rosenthal butcher shops and restaurants. The Nazi Party blamed the Katz family for the court shutting down their publication for a stretch in 1928. With Hitler now in power, the Katz family would suffer revenge. Several Katz family members had served in the German army honorably during World War I. The family was assimilated into German society and dedicated to Cologne, having lived in the Rhineland for six generations.[21] Their circle of friends included a large group of German Christians. They did not believe the Nazis would be able to last long actually governing Germany.

But in the middle of March, the editor of *Westdeutscher Beobachter* announced the illegal removal of Cologne Mayor Adenauer from his office, and the Katzes' feelings dramatically shifted. The boycott of Jewish businesses, which was unveiling at that same time, affected them directly because of the interference of SA troops in Jewish-operated butcher shops. The Katz family was shocked by the aggressively organized national boycott of Jewish businesses.[22]

On April 1, 1933, the Nazis posted demeaning antisemitic banners on many Jewish businesses. Uniformed members of the SA stood next to the doorways of almost every Jewish merchant to prevent Germans from entering the store. While the SA in the 1920s was originally made up of former German soldiers, by the 1930s, it appealed to young Germans who did not qualify to enter the German army, which was allowed to only have 100,000 soldiers.[23] SA members wanted to be true soldiers, and massive groups marched through the streets of Cologne, carrying signs demanding that citizens stay away from Jewish shops. The SA troops passed out leaflets and chanted humiliations of Jews. They had trucks with loudspeakers blasting a call forbidding Germans to buy from Jews. The SA photographed customers who ignored the Nazi's words and went to Jewish stores were photographed by the SA and classified as betrayers of Germany. The Nazi SA pulled two members of the Katz family, Benno and son Arnold, from their butcher shop and forced them to march through the streets of Cologne carrying a sign that read, "Don't buy from Jews."

Other Katz family members, Carl and Helmut, thought they could intimidate the SA guard standing next to their butcher shop. Still, there were too many SA soldiers on their street, so they closed their shop to prevent any escalation of difficulty.[24] A lot of non-Jews followed the Nazis' order for the boycott. However, a significant number of lower working-class people did show up, especially to stores carrying items they needed, such as butcher shops. It is possible these were workers who supported the Communist Party. Among the Jewish business owners in Cologne, many did not even open their stores. Some who did open stayed inside, waiting for customers. Many Jews felt they just had to conciliate the Nazis through cooperative, calm behavior. Uncle Richard took none of those approaches.

Like most of Cologne's Jews, Uncle Richard knew the boycott was coming. But his approach and preparations were completely different from the bulk of the Jewish community.

"I cannot be silent," he told his friends and family.

As a strong believer in the Social Democratic Party and the actual civil laws of the Weimar Republic, Uncle Richard felt he had the legal right to protest the actions of the Nazi Party. He did not want to stay silent while the Jewish people were being abused, nor ignore the undermining of the Republic. Naturally, he felt that other Jews should come together with him to protest, but too many Jewish leaders believed that finding a way to cooperate with the Nazi government would protect German Jews. They were afraid to take an open stand against Nazi oppression of the Jewish people, so Uncle Richard was largely alone in his commitment to protest.

He believed, like many German Jews, that the Nazi government would be temporary. From studying German and German-Jewish history, Uncle Richard knew there were high and low points of antisemitism. Having witnessed, as an adult, the constant overturning of Reichstag majorities through continuous elections, he felt his taking a stand would help push the population's feelings in the proper direction. He knew that the Nazi Party respected the German military, so he believed that his being a recipient of the Iron Cross in World War I would prevent personal harm.

While he did not have any fellow Jews join or help with his protest, he did work with his Catholic brother-in-law, Heinz Flogerhover, the printer who lived next door to him. Heinz had already dealt with some Nazi intrusion into his business, as they assumed it was a Jewish business. However, he was able to at least confuse them by stating he was Catholic, not Jewish. Heinz took care of two items for Uncle Richard. First, he printed a leaflet Uncle Richard wrote that he planned to pass out from the doorway of his shop. Second, Heinz took the photograph of Uncle Richard that became part of German-Jewish history—his standing in the doorway next to a Nazi SA soldier. Uncle Richard wanted this day of injustice to the Jewish people to be permanently recorded.

Uncle Richard stood in the doorway of his store wearing his Iron Cross. He had a slightly sardonic smile. He was a true patriotic German war veteran. He believed his status as a decorated veteran would be an effective counter to the Nazis' approach. He knew that most Germans respected fellow citizens who were frontline veterans from World War I. He stood next to a young SA member whose commitment to the German military was a combination of fake and racist, as opposed to Uncle Richard's, which was based on true military service for the country. Like many German-Jewish war veterans, he saw the young SA members as inferior to those who truly experienced the war. Therefore, despite the presence of the SA, Uncle Richard was not afraid to distribute his anti-Nazi leaflets.

"To all front buddies and Germans!" the leaflet began. "Our Reich Chancellor Hitler and ministers Frick and Goring have repeatedly declared as follows: 'Anyone insulting a combat veteran is punishable by imprisonment!'" Next, his leaflet listed how his brother served in the German army for the full war, how he served in the last year and a half and received the Iron Cross second class for his bravery "in the face of the enemy." He included that his father, who was already ailing at age 58, was in the auxiliary. He then pushed this perspective:

"With this record in the service of the nation as a good German, must we allow ourselves to be publicly insulted? Should that be the thanks of the fatherland, that the press and radio urge sixty-five million Germans not to buy from German Jews, and that every German Jew, even the smallest merchant or artisan is to be boycotted? Has the German Jew become a **second class human**, only to be tolerated as a guest in his fatherland?

We see this action against German Judaism as an insult to the memory of **12,000 German combat soldiers of the Jewish faith killed in action.**

We also see in this action an insult to every decent citizen. We trust that even today there is in Cologne still the civil courage that Bismarck called for, and German loyalty in support of us Jews."

He signed the leaflet as "Combat Veteran Richard Stern."

Uncle Richard handed the leaflet to anyone passing by his store, including the SA soldier who stood next to him. The Nazi Party had a newspaper station at 22 Marsilstein, next door to the Stern bedding store. This provided rapid communication to the Nazi press, resulting in increased danger to Uncle Richard. Indeed, the Nazis who read his pamphlet did not see it as justification to properly treat Jewish war veterans. Rather, they simply saw it as Jews trying to disgrace the Nazi Party. About an hour after he gave the leaflet to the SA soldier next to his doorway, Uncle Richard was arrested by an SS soldier.

The Gestapo came into existence just a few weeks later, so Nazis ran no official prison. Uncle Richard was taken to one of the local police headquarters. As a result of Hitler's order for local police around Germany to form a working relationship with the SA and SS, a significant number of city police felt they must become members of the Nazi Party. Uncle Richard was forced to sit in the police station. He felt nervous. Then a police officer, who had already joined the Nazi Party but knew Uncle Richard fairly well, approached him.

"What are you doing here?" he asked.

"They arrested me," Uncle Richard answered.

"You better get out of here."

He saw Uncle Richard as a friend because they were both German war veterans. He took him to the back of the police station to escape through the back door. At that moment, the focus of Uncle Richard's life had to change from resistance to survival.

The boycott of Jewish businesses technically continued for three days. It turned out that Uncle Richard was the only Jewish protester in Cologne.[25] While he had no official leadership position in the Jewish community, his decision to protest made him a symbolic, moral leader.

Today in Cologne, the EL DE Hause Museum gives the history of National Socialism in the city. Its building was the headquarters and prison of the Gestapo. Their research found that Uncle Richard was the only Jewish protester against the boycott in Cologne. In the museum section illustrating the fate of Cologne Jews, there are two pictures from the boycott on April 1, 1933. One is of the two Katz family members forced to march in the streets. The other is Uncle Richard standing in his doorway, protesting next to a member of the SA.

Until I was about seven years old, Uncle Richard had a dog named Curly. When we would visit him in Allentown, I would go with him on Curly's walks. On each one, he would tell me some kind of silly dog story. The one I remember is about Curly's best friend, a groundhog. He told me how Curly and the groundhog loved to play with each other, even though Curly barked and the groundhog did not. We walked along undeveloped properties near his house and came to a hole in the ground in which I am pretty sure a groundhog lived. It did not come out, so I had no idea how much of what Uncle Richard had told me was literal or just imaginative. I knew he liked to create stories, but here was a hole in the ground that Curly was sniffing around. Was Curly really friends with an animal so different from him? A groundhog? Today, it strikes me how Uncle Richard was a friend with someone so different from him, a policeman who was a member of the Nazi Party, yet kept him out of prison after being pulled from his doorway and arrested.

The pamphlet Uncle Richard passed out when protesting

Richard Stern standing in the door of his store protesting the Nazi boycott of Jewish businesses (April 1, 1933). Next to him is a Nazi SA soldier. This picture is in numerous museums in Germany.

Richard Stern's cousins, Benno and Arnold Katz, forced to march with Nazi SA soldiers carrying a sign calling for Germans to boycott Jewish businesses (April 1, 1933)

1. Bracher, p 160
2. Idem, p 163
3. Idem, p 169
4. Craig, p 510

5. Idem, p 511
6. Idem, p 524
7. Idem, p 532
8. Idem, p 536
9. Idem, p 547
10. Bracher, p 181
11. Elon, p 387
12. Craig, p 548
13. Bracher, p 200
14. Elon, p 391
15. Bracher, p 202
16. Craig, p 578
17. Idem, p 572
18. Corbach, p 3
19. Idem, p 14
20. Idem, p 15
21. Vieten, p 109
22. Idem, p 110
23. Bracher, p 95
24. Idem, p 112
25. Evidence from Birte Klarzak.

6

JEWISH LIFE

In 1959, Uncle Richard wrote a brief summary of what he called his "messed up course of life." He did not describe any of his protest actions from April 1, 1933. Instead, he described how the boycott of Jewish businesses ruined the bedding store that had provided him with a good income. He told of his arrest by the SS, not even mentioning that his protest led to it. He then concluded with this admission: "I had underestimated the sense of the so-called National Socialist Movement." At 60 years old, he had a diminished outlook on the quality of his life. He did not focus on the moments that others would have considered heroic. Instead, he was disturbed by how his life had been degraded from a kind of normality to a focus on survival for my nana (his sister), my dad (his nephew), and himself. For my uncle, as for so many German Jews, each year of the 1930s increased Jewish denigration. The rise of the Nazis prevented him from what he mostly wanted—to enjoy a simple, regular life.

One would think that the growth of Jewish persecution would have created unity within the Jewish community. It is understandable that, before Hitler's rise to power in early 1933, there were diverse political, cultural, and religious perspectives among the Jews. Having witnessed numerous changes in the government, along with the Weimar Republic's constitutional guarantee of civil rights, they were unable to predict what the post-Weimar world after April 1, 1933, would truly be. There were some Jews who tried to escape Germany early in Hitler's reign. The bulk of those who left from Cologne were doctors, academics, or from the upper class. Yet many Jews continued to believe Hitler's power could not last long, and Germany would return to normal. Further, while most German Jews supported the republic and its more liberal political parties, others actually observed and absorbed the Nazi Party's politics differently from the reality for the Jewish people. Numerically, they were a tiny minority, but they were outspoken in their attempts to convince others to agree with their beliefs.

During the months and first couple of years after the boycott, Uncle Richard's feelings drifted back and forth. On the one hand, he focused on earning enough money to take care of his sister and her son. He understood the evil of the Nazi Party and thought about trying to get out of Germany. On the other hand, he thought of himself as a patriotic German who loved Cologne. He did not feel easy with trying to start a new life in a different country. He did not know any foreign language. Uncle Richard was very aware of what was unfolding in Germany. He was aware of the range of thoughts in the Jewish world about the best way to approach Nazism. But it was his nephew, my dad, who was living through and witnessing the clash of different Jewish reactions to Nazism while going to school.

Although a small group, the conservative, pro-nationalist German Jews were organized and vocal. In February of 1933, a youthful, anti-Zionist group formed an organization called *Deutscher Vortrupp* (D.V.).[1] They were led by a young author and historian, Dr. Hans Joachim Schoeps, who did not support the Weimar Republic. He wanted a return to a monarchy.[2] Schoeps, along with the members of the D.V., would not acknowledge the true depth of the Nazi Party's antisemitism. Instead, they saw the central purpose of the Nazi Party as re-establishing the strength of German nationalism through reviving the nation's economy and military.[3] The D.V. was focused on transforming the Jewish community along conservative lines. Just before the April 1, 1933 boycott of Jewish businesses, they joined with other conservative Jewish groups to express loyalty to Germany.[4] Even after the boycott, the D.V. looked at Nazi antisemitism as minor, praising how the Nazis gave Germans an alternative to liberalism and Communism.[5] Some right-wing Jews justified their early support of Hitler through their opposition to the presence of many Eastern European Jews who fled to Germany because of either the Russian pogroms in the late 19th century or World War I.

Zionism presented one of the most significant conflicts between right-wing and left-wing Jews. During the first Zionist Congress in 1897, only 16 of the 207 delegates came from Germany.[6] The weak support among German Jews for Zionism continued until a new, more radical generation developed from 1909 onward.[7] In the early 1930s, a small group of German Jews began immigrating to Palestine. While support for Zionism grew, it was not a universally endorsed belief among German Jews. However, Zionist groups represented an extremely different perspective on the situation for German Jews than right wing groups like the D.V. Zionists recognized the threats and believed Jewish immigration to Palestine was a good solution. Right-wing Jewish groups opposed the Zionist's efforts to recruit Jewish youth.[8]

When the Nazis took power and began taking governmental action against the Jewish people, Dad attended the same elementary school that Uncle Richard attended as a child. It was a Jewish school overseen by the state. Some teachers were still strict German types. Their methods of discipline were old-school and hard, often striking the students with bamboo sticks. They conducted their classes "by the letter" to ensure that all was being done under the state's education rules in case authorities checked up on them. These teachers also tended to physically punish students they perceived not only as misbehaving but not learning properly.

Other teachers were quite different. One teacher, Dr. Brown, who taught Dad through a large group of classes during his elementary school years, was a Zionist. He took trips to Palestine in the summers of 1933, 1934, and 1935. Upon his return, Dr. Brown would share stories about life in Palestine with his students. This teacher's experience influenced Dad's desire to immigrate to Palestine. Dr. Brown did not handle students the same way as the strictest teachers. Instead of physical punishment, he would have them stand in a corner or assign them additional homework. Dr. Brown eventually immigrated to Palestine, and Dad found him during his own first trip to Israel in 1969.

By the time of the boycott, Dad had already been in school four years. Even at only 10 years old, he was aware of the situation beginning to affect the Jewish community. The leadership of the school required the students to sing German songs constantly. Even though they were not Nazi songs, this was clearly an attempt to show the Nazi government how these young Jews were patriotic. By the time they reached 11 years old, Dad and his friends had objected to the number of German songs they were forced to sing and requested more Hebrew and Jewish songs.

Dad's school had about 1,000 students. By 1934, a large range of political groups operated in the school, running from the far right, represented by the Jewish Veteran's Youth Movement, to the far left, including *Hashomer Hatzair*, a socialist Zionist youth movement. All of these groups were pushing to recruit students. Because Uncle Richard was a war veteran, Dad decided to join the Jewish Veteran's Youth Movement. It took him about six months to become disgusted with this group, as he felt they were imitating the Nazi youth movement, wearing black boots, black pants, and white shirts while expressing support for the German government. Dad then joined a left-wing Zionist movement, which shortly after he joined, merged with *Hashomer Hatzair*. The Zionist groups were always in conflict with the right-wing Jewish movements in Dad's elementary school.

In *Hashomer Hatzair*, Dad began training for immigration to Palestine, most likely to a kibbutz. His best friend, Harry Mandel, was also a member of this Zionist group. He was the son of Polish Jews who had come to Germany years earlier. The young leader of his group was Jupshin Proter, who eventually did move to Palestine, changing his name to Josef Porat. He served in a Jewish military company for the British, doing intelligence work. When the state of Israel was declared independent in 1948, Josef Porat was an early member of the *Mossad*. Despite the conflicts with right-wing Jewish groups and the rise of the Nazis, Dad's memories of his time in *Hashomer Hatzair* during the mid-1930s felt good. He loved the meetings, singing, and summer camp events. All of this helped him develop dedication to the establishment of a Jewish state where he could live.

While Dad was experiencing the dramatic changes in Germany through activities in his school, Uncle Richard dealt with a sharp decline in his bedding-store business. He could no longer employ workers as before, so Nana began to help him in the store when needed. He witnessed the attacks on larger Jewish businesses, such as department stores. However, during the first few months after the boycott, he still hoped there would be a limit to the Nazi regime, perhaps because the smaller Jewish businesses were left alone. Like many Jews, he now kept quiet, despite incidents of Jewish persecution. Instead of enjoying the *Karneval* as it passed in front of his shop and getting involved, Uncle Richard now stayed out of public exposure.

One exception to Uncle Richard's increased privacy was his continued involvement in the *Reichsbund Jüdischer Frontsoldaten*, a Jewish war veterans' organization. He helped organize a commemoration for 11,000 Jewish soldiers on July 8, 1934. This included an unveiling ceremony at Roonstrasse Synagogue for a memorial to deceased soldiers, with 500 in attendance. Years after the war, the memorial was moved to the cemetery under the care of the rebuilt Roonstrasse Synagogue. Today, a prayer is said for the veterans every year right before Rosh Hashanah. Uncle Richard was able to continue donating to the *Reichsbund Jüdischer Frontsoldaten* until the end of 1936. By that time, the pressure on the Jewish population had significantly increased through new persecution laws, plus the Nazis' total elimination of any opposing political groups.

In truth, the result of the original act against Jewish businesses in 1933 did not achieve what Hitler had hoped. On March 26 of that year, he said to Goebbels, "the foreign Jews will think better of the matter when their racial comrades in Germany begin to get it in the neck".[9] The boycott failed to have the effect Hitler wanted because German businesses overall were still very fragile, and all businesses were still needed. The SA attacks on Jewish shops hurt other businesses in the same area. However, constant hatred of Jews occupied Hitler's mind, being a central focus of the Nazi Party. While Jewish businesses were allowed to continue, the focus turned to limiting Jewish rights in every other area. This would take a few years longer but result in the violent, total domination of Jews that Hitler wanted.

The Stern family experienced a step-by-step, year-by-year increasing shutdown of Jewish life. Jewish businesses were not immediately all closed, especially smaller ones, because their complete absence would negatively affect other German businesses in the same districts.[10] However, the Aryanization of Jewish businesses did begin, increasing bit by bit each year in the 1930s. In Cologne, many Jewish business owners were forced to sell to Germans for a low price. It took a growing series of oppressive Nazi rules to transform Germany into what Hitler preferred. Some were very specifically focused on the Jews.

From the beginning of Nazism's rise, the judicial system was continuously undermined. In March 1933, the Nazis created their first concentration camps. Even in the earliest years of the Third Reich, if a court found a political opponent or a Jew not guilty of a crime, that person was usually transferred to a concentration camp, not set free.[11] The judges themselves were handled delicately, but it was the attorneys who the Nazis felt must be servants of their movement. So in April of 1933, a law was issued imposing strict racial and political qualifications for lawyers.[12] On the same day, the Civil Service Act removed Jews and anyone suspected of not supporting the Nazi Party from the government or civil positions.[13] The Nazis absorbed trade unions by forming an organization to oversee the functions of labor groups to keep them powerless.[14]

Perhaps the most potent law solidifying Nazi power came on July 14, 1933. The Nazi Party was declared the only legal political party in Germany. Anyone who tried to continue the work of a former party or create a new one would serve a three-year prison sentence.[15]

In addition, there were laws issued that focused more specifically on Jewish degradation. In April of 1933, a law was issued against overcrowding in schools of higher learning.[16] This prevented Jews from accessing education beyond elementary school. In July of 1933, naturalizations of Eastern European Jews who had become German citizens were revoked along with any other people who were considered to be "undesirable."[17] At the end of September 1933, a new law kicked Jews out of the institutions of theater, music, and arts.[18] Hitler's successes in foreign affairs resulted in antisemitic actions. In January 1935, he repudiated the clauses in the Versailles Treaty limiting Germany's military arms. The expansion of the German military began in March 1935 with the creation of 36 new army divisions. On May 21, 1935, the Defense Act was declared, subjecting all German males under 45 to being called into the military, including reserve units. As second-class citizens, the German Jews would not be called into the military.[19] The joyful reaction of faithful Nazis was a set of attacks on Jewish property and their personal rights.[20]

The full official legalization of antisemitism took place with the passing of the Nuremberg Laws by the Reichstag on September 15, 1935.[21] They contained two segments that set the stage for the dramatically rising Jewish persecution until the end of World War II.

The first, "Reich Citizenship Law," declared the Reich would protect only a subject of the state. Then, article 2 included these three statements:

1. A Reich citizen is a subject of the state who is of German or related blood and proves by his conduct that he is willing and fit to faithfully serve the German people and Reich.
2. Reich citizenship is acquired through the granting of a Reich citizenship certificate.
3. The Reich citizen is the sole bearer of full political rights in accordance with the law.

Officials appointed by the Nazi government issued the citizenship certificate. The second segment established legal racism. It was called "Law for the Protection of German Blood and German Honor." It forbade Jews from marrying German citizens as well as extramarital relations between Jews and German citizens. It also prohibited Jews from employing female Germans in their homes. Jews were banned from flying either the German or Nazi flags.

By the middle of 1938, the Jewish people were almost completely shut out of German life. In addition to all the previously engaged antisemitic laws and actions, Jews were no longer admitted to restaurants, pharmacies, and most schools. They were not eligible for governmental aid. There were a large number of amendments to the Nuremberg laws from 1935 to 1938, constantly worsening Jewish discrimination.[22] This included a requirement to carry identity cards or passports containing the stereotypical middle name of either Israel or Sarah.

There was one brief period in which the heaviness of Jewish oppression let up a bit. It was during the Olympics in Berlin from August 1-16, 1936. German-Jewish athletes were banned from participating in the games. Some countries held back Jewish participants to keep from offending the Germans. But the Nazi government held back on antisemitic actions at the time of the Olympics to display a better impression of the Third Reich to other countries. Uncle Richard and Dad followed the Olympics on the radio. By this point, they were not rooting for the Germans, but the Americans, and Dad followed the track and field competitions that featured Jesse Owens, who became his favorite athlete that summer. When the Olympic games were done, fun was squashed for the Stern family until they left Germany in the middle of 1939.

The changes in Jewish life personally struck Dad in 1937, when he had his bar mitzvah, which symbolizes entering adulthood in Judaism, in the Gluckengasse Synagogue. His Torah portion was from the very beginning of Deuteronomy. Dad still had his "boy soprano" voice for his bar mitzvah, losing it just a couple of weeks later. Despite the increased persecution of Jews through laws forbidding them from so much of German society, the synagogues in Cologne were still operating. So the tradition of chanting Torah for a bar mitzvah was joyful for Dad, his mom, and Uncle Richard. The difficulty of 1937 came from the law prohibiting Jews from entering higher learning.

When Dad was finished with elementary school, he would have loved to study engineering in a German school. His only choice, however, was to enroll in the Jewish trade school. The training subjects offered were auto mechanics, carpentry, machinery mechanics, metal trade, and woodworking. They taught girls as well, but in subjects such as needle trade and cooking. The school was a training ground for living in Israel, so the learning included evening classes in Hebrew. Considering the various trade choices, Dad preferred to study to be a machinist. Even at 13 years old, he had an affinity for diagnosing and fixing broken machinery.

However, Dad enrolled in training for woodworking, in particular, building cabinetry. This choice was urged by Uncle Richard. A good friend of the family named Lottinger was the woodworking/cabinetry teacher. He had been in charge of coordinating and building all of the stage carpentry for the Cologne opera house. He was tossed out of the position after the Nazis issued the law in September of 1933 kicking Jews out of art institutions. For the first year, Dad took what was considered a pre-apprenticeship class in the building of the Jewish Children's Home on Lützowstrasse. He then attended the official trade school on Utrechter Strasse. It turned out that Mr. Lottinger was an excellent teacher, and Dad attributed his future talent as a cabinetmaker to him.

The 1935 Nuremberg laws created difficulty for so many of Uncle Richard's friends and family. His friends' businesses fell apart as the Nazis "Aryanized" Jewish businesses. The Katz family faced numerous problems. Some were being pushed by the Nazi government to pay unfair taxes. The butcher shops no longer operated at a profit because they were denied access to good quality meat to sell in addition to diminishing non-Jewish customers. Several members had already moved out of Germany to Belgium and Holland. Uncle Richard's cousin Henni's older son, Helmut, moved to South Africa, along with some other butchers who felt it was a decent way to get away from German restrictions on their businesses.[23]

Uncle Richard's Catholic brother-in-law, Heinz Flogerhover, had been fighting the accusation of having a Jewish business even though he could prove he was not Jewish. Yet his business still suffered damage when a Nazi smashed his windows. Given the Nuremberg law of 1935 forbidding the marriage of Germans to Jews, Heinz could have had a great excuse to get away from suffering by leaving his wife, Uncle Richard's oldest sister, Thekla. However, Heinz was a far better quality person, caring deeply for his wife and two daughters. He was dedicated not only to those family members but to his Jewish in-laws as well. Like Heinz demonstrated when he assisted Uncle Richard's protest on April 1, 1933, he would never support the Nazis.

By 1937, Uncle Richard only had Jewish clientele. Further, many of his best Jewish customers had emigrated or were trying to emigrate from Germany. So Uncle Richard changed what he was selling into items needed by emigrants. These included folding beds, suitcases, and trunks. In order to protect his business more, in January 1938, he moved it to the second floor. He then rented the first floor to a Jewish merchant named Homberg, who installed a hat shop. The Stern family had been able to keep somewhat functioning until the events of 1938 created a completely new reality.

Like many German-Jewish war veterans, Uncle Richard had non-Jewish friends who tried to help his family, at least in the first period of Nazi power. As a front-line veteran, he did not feel Hitler's rule would last long at the beginning of the Nazi Party's rise in power. To Uncle Richard's dismay, the process of his total rejection as a valued German army veteran began in late 1933. It had been discovered that he was eligible to receive the Hanseatic Cross, a special medal given to World War I divisions formed in the cities of Hamburg, Bremen, and Lubeck. He did not receive it years earlier as he had come from Cologne but being placed into the division qualified him. However, when the new Nazi government found he was Jewish, he was denied this medal. By the end of 1933, the Nazi-led government declared that Jewish officers had not fought properly. In May of 1935, the Military Service Law prohibited military service from anyone not considered of true German descent.

Uncle Richard's sense of German patriotism certainly ended completely on April 1, 1938. He was physically examined at the Cologne military recruiting station. While it was concluded he was physically fit, the real bottom line was an official statement that he could not register to join the military. Rather, he had to register with the police to be overseen as a potential offender. This conclusion was based on a certificate issued to him by the Cologne police a year earlier, March 1937, which stated, "Since he, as a Jew, is not enlisted to active military service, he is being removed from his acceptance in the personnel roster." Any possible respect as a decorated German war veteran was completely over. Uncle Richard was now only considered to be a typical criminal Jew. He was absolutely afraid of being arrested and sent to a concentration camp, yet his heart still drove him to do something out of his dedication to his fellow Jews, especially after Hitler ordered an extremely aggressive action against a group of Jews.

On March 12, 1938, Hitler and his cohorts convinced the leaders of Austria to open their borders to German troops. At the same time, Austrian National Socialists took control of the Austrian government.[24] Within a few days, the *Anschluss*, the annexation of

Austria by Germany, was complete. For Austrian Jews, the resulting persecution was immediately far more radical than that suffered by Germany's Jews. Many Austrian Jews fled, with a significant number coming to Cologne because that part of the Rhineland was close to the borders of Belgium and Holland.

Uncle Richard could no longer outwardly perform anti-Nazi actions. However, his home quickly became known as a "safe haven" for Jews fleeing from Austria, and later on also the more oppressive German cities of Nuremberg and Munich. Uncle Richard tried to do as much as he could to help those fellow Jews running from the severe persecution after the *Anschluss*. He harbored them, fed them, and assisted their attempts to cross the border out of Germany. Many of the border crossings he assisted were technically illegal. Uncle Richard, Dad, and Nana heard story after story of the atrocities inflicted upon the Austrian Jews that caused them to panic and run. Within the first week of the *Anschluss*, Jews suffered from violent brutality, destroyed businesses, and plundered homes. The outright violence lessened after a week, but in April, thousands of Jewish students were placed in segregated schools. On May 20, 1938, the Nazi government officially applied the Nuremberg laws to Austrian Jews.

While the violent life in Cologne had been hard, they were shocked by the persecution stories told to them by the Jewish refugees they hosted from Vienna and other Austrian towns. This resulted in something beyond Uncle Richard's attempts to help Nazi victims. It was a turning point for his approach to life in Cologne. He finally realized what the ensuing fate for German Jews, thus the fate for his own family, was doomed to be.

In the summer of 1938, Uncle Richard went to the American consulate in Stuttgart to register an application for emigration visas to the United States. He submitted it for himself, his sister Martha, and my dad, who had just turned 15 years old. American immigration laws placed a quota of about 26,000 for German immigrants. By late 1938 the number of Germans applying for immigration had grown to over 150,000. His early application at the American Consulate was extremely lucky, as their application numbers were low enough to receive visas after getting someone in the United States to sponsor them and pledge to cover the immigrants' living cost if necessary. In August 1938, a law was issued forcing Jews to use the names of *Israel* for a man and *Sara* for a woman as middle names. They were put into the passports of Uncle Richard, Martha, and Dad.

Despite hearing about the suffering of Austrian Jews, experiencing his dismissal from being a soldier, the increased oppression suffered by his sister and nephew, and even after submitting the applications for American visas, Uncle Richard was still hesitant about leaving Cologne. It was a combination of reasons. One, he still loved and felt the obligation of being with his friends and family in Cologne. He also felt the need to do what he could for other Jews with the assets he still had. Finally, he was hesitant about starting a completely new life in another country. He was doubtful and scared of his ability to learn another language. Uncle Richard, like most other folks, could not have predicted what would happen next: *Kristallnacht*. His application for American visas started out as a precaution but turned out to save Dad's and Nana's lives as well as his own.

---

1. Rheins, p 207
2. Idem, p 208
3. Idem, p 210
4. Idem, p 216
5. Idem, p 217
6. Elon, p 289
7. Idem, p 290
8. Rheins, p 220
9. Craig, p 632
10. Idem, p 633
11. Bracher, p 214
12. Craig, p 580
13. Bracher, p 197
14. Craig, p 583
15. Idem, p 582
16. Idem, p 633
17. Idem, p 634
18. Cologne During National Socialism, p 186

19. Rheins, p 223
20. Craig, p 634
21. Bracher, p 253
22. Idem, p 366
23. Vieten, p 147
24. Bracher, p 309

7

BROKEN DISHES

In May 1973, Dad and I traveled to Israel on a special father-and-son trip. While there, we visited Josef Porat, who had been his *Hashomer Hatzair* leader when he lived in Germany. That is when I learned that Porat, whose original German name was Jupshin Proter, had been in Israeli intelligence, an original member of the Mossad, after serving in British intelligence during World War II. I also learned that he was married to Orna Porat, then a famous Israeli actress. But the most emotional moment came when Mr. Porat showed Dad a photo album with pictures featuring many of their activities from *Hashomer Hatzair*.

Dad turned a page, stopped, and turned pale. There was a picture of him having a fake swordfight with another member. Dad turned to Mr. Porat and said this was his best friend as a teenager, Harry Mandel, whose family had come to Germany from Poland. The Mandels were kicked out of Germany in late October 1938. Dad walked with his friend and the Mandel family to the train station to say goodbye, believing he would never see him again. He did not even know if Harry was alive. Mr. Porat, in a quiet voice, told Dad that Harry was alive and living close by in Tel Aviv. He gave Dad Harry's phone number.

The next day, while I saw a friend from a trip to Israel two years earlier, Dad met with the best friend he had not seen in 35 years. Dad did not speak Hebrew and Harry did not speak English, so they spoke in German. To me, at 19 years old, this was an example of how fantastic it was to be in Israel, to see Jewish survivors in a Jewish country. What I had not yet learned was the real story of how the predicament of Polish Jews in Germany launched the sequence of events that led to *Kristallnacht*.

Between Germany and Austria, there were about 50,000 Jews of Polish origin.[1] They suffered an even deeper level of Jewish persecution from the Nazis than the average German Jew. There was even a number of ultraconservative German Jews, such as members of the *Deutscher Vortrupp*, who did not like the presence of any Eastern European Jews. The Polish government was also antisemitic. It was resistant to allowing these Jews to return while the pressure against them in Germany kept increasing.[2]

On March 31, 1938, the Polish government issued a law revoking the Polish passports of anyone living abroad for more than five years. This law was to take effect on October 31, 1938.[3] The German government did not want to be stuck with 15,000 stateless Jews who would not be admitted to another country, so it decided to act quickly to expel Polish Jews from Germany.

Starting on October 28, Polish Jews were forced to go to police stations or railway stations. They were allowed only one suitcase per person and were given a gratuity of ten marks to travel out of Germany on train cars with bolted doors and armed escorts.[4]

This transportation was kind of a preview of how Jews would later be taken to death camps. The 15,000 stateless Polish Jews: men, women, and children, were forced onto trains from numerous key German cities, including Cologne. There were hundreds just in Cologne, including the Mandel family, who had lived there for decades. On October 29, 1938, Dad walked with the Mandels to the Cologne train station, helping them carry the family's luggage. Dad was terribly upset that his best friend was being kicked out of Germany. It was impossible for Dad to know what the expulsion of his friend and his fellow Polish Jews would lead to.

Living in Paris was a young Polish Jew, Herschel Grynszpan, whose family lived in Hannover, Germany. On November 3, 1938, he received a letter from his sister telling him how the police forced the family to leave Germany and the details of the nasty oppression.[5] Grynszpan intended to apply for a longer residency permit because his legal residency in Paris had expired, and he loved living there. But when he received his sister's letter, he abandoned any concern about his residency and focused on taking vengeance against the Germans for what happened to his family.[6] Grynszpan's plan was to buy a gun and kill the German ambassador in Paris. He bought a pistol and, on Monday, November 7, went to the German embassy, then asked to see an official. He was brought to third secretary Ernst vom Rath's office. Vom Rath asked if Grynszpan had an important document to give him. Grynszpan responded, "You are a filthy *boche* and here, in the name of twelve thousand persecuted Jews, is your document," and then shot him five times.[7]

The German newspaper headlines focused on a Jew being responsible for the shooting. Now 15 years old, Dad read the propaganda articles that said this was a case of Jews trying to do away with Germans. Dad was in his trade school's Tuesday night Hebrew class on November 8, 1938. His teacher was a liberal rabbi, Dr. Adolf Kober, who had a long history of leading Jewish education in Cologne. He was a founder of the school for adult Jewish education, *Jüdisches Lehrhaus* (Jewish Training House), in 1928 and was a known scholar on German-Jewish history. To his Hebrew class on November 8, Dr. Kober stated, "All pray tonight that vom Rath lives, because if he dies, God help us." The next day, Wednesday, November 9, at 4:30 in the afternoon, vom Rath died. Dr. Kober seemed to know exactly what was about to happen.

Leading up to *Kristallnacht*, actions were already beginning against Jewish institutions, private businesses, and homes on November 8, a day before vom Rath's death. Local leaders of the Nazi Party held meetings where "Jewish crimes" were denounced. Attacks began on local synagogues and businesses.[8] It is clear how the full pogrom beginning on November 9, after vom Rath died, was an existing strategy; it was probably coordinated by Joseph Goebbels.[9] By the evening of November 9, the attacks against synagogues exploded. In Cologne, the major ones, including Roonstrasse and Glockengasse, were set on fire and all the doors and windows were smashed.[10] Even the synagogue in the small town of Friesheim, built by Uncle Richard's great grandfather, Seligmann Stern, was destroyed. As November 9th turned to the 10th, attacks began on private Jewish businesses and homes throughout Germany. Uncle Richard, Nana, and Dad all lived through this. Like all German Jews, they shared this pogrom. Everyone had different experiences, but all absorbed the same horror.

Dad and Nana immediately hid in Heinz and Thekla Flogerhover's home, which was next door to Uncle Richard's. Their print shop was on the ground floor, with living quarters upstairs. The two buildings' walls were connected, creating a double wall over two feet thick. Connecting the two homes was a one-inch-thick pipe that the two families called a "telephone." In Uncle Richard's house, the pipe came out on the stairway. In the Flogerhover's home, it was in the kitchen. Dad stood next to the pipe in his Aunt Thekla's kitchen to listen and try to look through. He saw some of what happened and heard the bulk of the destruction. The store and the second floor were both destroyed. The bedding store inventory, kept in the back of what was now mostly a hat shop, was ripped apart and thrown into the street. When they went up to the living room floor, dining room, and kitchen, the attack became personal. All the windows were smashed. Dishes were pulled out of the cabinets and shattered. Their food was thrown all over the floor. In the living room, like many Jewish families, they had a bust of Napoleon, as Napoleon was seen as a liberator of German Jews at the beginning of the 19th century. They broke it apart on the floor. Anything of value in Uncle Richard's home was stolen, including much of their clothing. Dad ended up with only one coat. As the weather in early November was already cold, their house became hard to stay in until the windows were fixed or boarded up. As he watched and listened, Dad's heart broke over the destruction of the home where he grew up.

Dad noticed SA troops dressed in civilian clothing, so he concluded they were the destroyers of Uncle Richard's store and home. The reality that the attackers were ununiformed SA or SS troops can be confirmed by a speech given by Goebbels in Munich, November 9. The attending party leaders understood Goebbels did not want the pogrom to look like the Nazi Party organized it.[11] The Jewish victims had already suffered so much from the SA and SS that the civilian disguise hardly fooled anyone.

The bedding thrown onto the street blocked the way of a nearby tram, so Uncle Richard's neighbors threw the inventory back into the first floor. It seemed the non-Jewish residents on Marsilstein cared more about the traffic continuing to move than the violence against their Jewish neighbors. Once the pogrom on their street was over later that Thursday morning, everyone was afraid to go back into the house through the front door. The Stern and Flogerhover houses had joint back yards, so Dad crawled on his belly, across the back yards, through the gate to their own back door, to avoid detection by the SA, since the curtains of the smashed windows were torn down, making everything visible. When he entered the house, Dad saw the complete destruction of their living area. It looked like a tornado had hit, but Dad had witnessed that humans did this to them.

Nana, Dad's mother, had a serious problem. She had been dealing with gall bladder difficulties and had some kind of stress attack while the SA was invading and destroying their home. Dad and his mother's sister, Thekla, could not tell if Nana's suffering was because of the bladder, a heart attack, or possibly a psychological breakdown. Given the severity of the pogrom, there was no way to get her to a doctor.

During the violence of *Kristallnacht*, Uncle Richard was not with the family very long. After his sister and Dad fled to the Flogerhover's house next door, he waited in the store, watching the attacks unfold. He was trying to figure out a way to protect the house. He saw the civilian-dressed SA and SS troops attack other

Jewish homes as well as a butcher shop right across from his store. He knew the owner well, Max Marx. His store was called a "New Kosher Butcher Shop" because traditional kosher meat was no longer allowed in Germany. Marx strongly stood in front of his store, and the Nazis threw a rock that hit his head and knocked him out. Uncle Richard saw the SS take Max Marx away and assumed he would be taken to the concentration camp in Dachau, where arrested Jews had been sent since 1933. Uncle Richard boarded the front door. The SA began to destroy it with axes and wrecking bars, so he finally left through the back door and went to his sister Thekla's house through the backyard. When the pogrom was over, his cousin Henni's husband, Carl Katz, was arrested, and he watched the Gestapo take him away in a car. Uncle Richard was back in his ruined store by five o'clock that evening.

However, Uncle Richard did not stay at his home with Dad and Nana for a couple of nights. Instead, he fled to a friend's house on the outskirts of Cologne, where he hid for two days to avoid arrest. Dad actually thought Richard had been arrested and considered it a miracle that he returned after a few days. In a later letter to a family member, Richard described the impact of *Kristallnacht* this way, "In a few minutes, we had aged many years, but we also became more vigilant." The vigilance he meant was determination to condemn Nazi Germany, leave it, and find a way to oppose it. My uncle then wrote how so many men between 16 and 60 years old had been arrested and sent to Dachau. "Some others came back after four to six weeks, but not all. Some made it back in an urn, which could be redeemed for five marks."

On the following day, November 11, Dad got a call from his teacher, Mr. Lottinger. Young Jewish men and teenage boys were ordered to board up the synagogue. They gathered boards, hammers, and nails to work on the lower doors and windows of the Roonstrasse Synagogue. In addition to boarding doors, Dad did some cleanup inside the synagogue. In the sanctuary, he saw that the holy ark containing the Torah scrolls was not burned down. He wondered how the fire had been put out to preserve it. The synagogue had a huge organ in the sanctuary that was broken to pieces. Dad picked up a piece of an organ pipe and foolishly wanted to take it. His teacher stopped him and said, "No, if you are searched and it is found on you, you will be taken to a concentration camp." So much had happened in the past 36 hours. So much was destroyed. So many were arrested. One Jew in Cologne was killed.

Kristallnacht ferociously opened the door for Hitler's addiction to anti-Jewish terrorism. The pogrom had destroyed almost every synagogue in Germany, over 7,000 stores, and resulted in the arrest of over 30,000 prosperous Jews.[12] The "Aryanization" of Jewish businesses increased. It had officially begun in April of 1938. In the summer of 1938, Jewish doctors were forced to end their practices within three months, and lawyers had to do the same by November 30.[13] The expropriation of Jewish businesses increased after *Kristallnacht.* By the end of November, Jews not only lost the last of their property rights but were forbidden from entering theaters, concerts, museums, athletic fields, and public baths. Even worse was the order for Jews to give up homes and move together into "Jewish" houses, a first step toward ghettoization. Many were then placed into forced labor.[14] The Jewish community was required to pay one billion marks to repair the damage committed by the SA and SS.[15] By 1939, German Jews had been severely abused, stripped of their citizenship, and deprived of their means for making a living. The numbers of Jews pushing to leave Germany for any other country exploded.

During *Kristallnacht,* Dad's trade school was destroyed and permanently closed. Realizing his nephew needed to have some kind of work or trade training, Uncle Richard met with a non-Jewish friend who owned an upholstery frame shop operating off of a back alley in Cologne. He knew him through his prior membership in the Social Democratic Party. Even as a gentile, he was very anti-Nazi. He said to Uncle Richard, "Yes, Rudi has to do something. I'll take him in through the back. My workers are Communists and they will not say anything." Dad worked there for six months, until about a month before leaving Germany. He had to be paid in cash, so there would be no record of a Jew "illegally" working at this manufacturing shop. Later in life, Dad was unable to prove he had been employed in Germany and was denied a pension from the German government. The men he worked with were excellent. All were anti-Nazi. All knew that he was Jewish. No worker said a word about Dad being there.

The Cologne Jewish community was forced to repair a building the Nazis damaged right next to the Roonstrasse Synagogue to serve as a Jewish community center. They were now forbidden from going to plays, operas, and concerts. It was even difficult to walk through parks as only a few benches were marked as permitted for Jews. The Jewish Community Center was put together quickly. It had a large auditorium in which religious services were held. At other times the auditorium housed a play, a concert, or put up a screen for a movie. It also contained a restaurant. It needed all of these elements as it became the only place in Cologne where Jewish events of any kind could take place. It also housed the Jewish community's administration.

Along with his cabinet teacher and some other students, Dad built an *Aron haKodesh*, a holy ark that held Torah scrolls. Mr. Lottinger had a snapshot of the Torah ark in the Glockengasse Synagogue that had been completely burned down, so they made theirs a replica. During the first weeks after *Kristallnacht,* Dad and a friend took their tools and went to Jewish homes to repair any damaged furniture that was not fully destroyed.

As many Jewish families were forced from their homes to live with other Jews, Uncle Richard's house was one of the domestic "ghettos" in Cologne. At any one time, three or four families were living at 20 Marsilstein Street. Some families were transient, staying just a few days. Those families were usually on their way out of the country. Others, such as the Hombergs, who had opened the hat shop downstairs, lived there for months. By the end of 1938, Uncle Richard had to close his business, as its space was now officially "Aryanized." Entering 1939, life for Uncle Richard and his family had fallen to a depressed level he had never dreamed would happen.

After the pogrom, Jews were eager to leave Cologne. Uncle

Richard's sister, Hilde, and her husband, Ludwig, immigrated to the United States in 1937. Ludwig's family, the Walkers, had several members who already lived in New York. Some were even born there. Immediately after *Kristallnacht*, Uncle Richard reached out to any family members already in New York, including the Walkers, to provide an affidavit for him, Nana, and Dad, so they would qualify for an American visa. The affidavit required proof that immigrants would not need to apply to the American government for financial support. Two members of the Walker family, David and Robert, along with a distant cousin born in America, Gladys Stern, agreed to supply affidavits. It was extremely fortunate for my uncle and his family that he had submitted applications to the American consulate in Stuttgart earlier in 1938 because they were processed in the order of the application number. Uncle Richard's, Nana's, and Dad's applications had low numbers, so once family in New York agreed to provide affidavits, getting the visas went relatively easy. The initial plan was for all three of them to leave on the USS Manhattan on May 15, 1939, but his sister's papers lacked something the American consulate in Stuttgart needed, which resulted in a delay for Nana and Dad.

Another issue came up. For Dad to get permission from Germany to leave, he needed the signature of his biological father, Walter Romberg. At 15 years old, Dad had to go to his father's apartment on his own, as his mother refused to go. In the spring of 1939, Dad took the paperwork to Walter's apartment for him to sign. He was a bit nervous about meeting a father he had no memory of ever seeing. All Dad knew about his father was what the Stern family shared about him. Walter was now 45 years old. When Dad arrived, Walter invited him in and then apologized for never being around for his son, but then said he was very happy that his son was able to get out of Germany. Walter was not the nasty person portrayed by the Stern family, particularly Dad's mother. He wished Dad well. In only the few minutes he was with his father, Dad realized he would have liked to know a lot more about the Romberg side of his family. As he was leaving the apartment, Dad heard voices that sounded like little girls.

Dad did not realize the difficult life his biological father ended up living. At 39 years old in 1932, Walter finally married a Catholic woman, Margarethe. They had been together for a couple of years, conceiving their first child, Charlotte, born in March of 1932. Through the 1930s, he ended up with four children, two daughters and two sons. Once the Nazis took power in 1933, his poor ability to work in business got worse. He constantly received financial aid from his most successful brother, Carl. By the end of 1938, Walter was not allowed to have his own job or business but was placed into forced, almost slave labor, working on a government-supervised road crew. His humor was dark, as his life was in constant turmoil.

On *Kristallnacht,* Walter's apartment did not suffer an attack, probably because his wife was Catholic. Margarethe helped him get to work early the morning of November 10 to make sure he arrived safely. They saw that a Jewish-owned business next door to their apartment building had been attacked. Later, their older children saw SA troops come back, some in uniform and some in civilian clothing, to fully destroy the business with axes and crowbars. Across the street from the business was a small Jewish prayer room, and the SA men went in, pulled out the Torah, and threw it onto the street. Unlike his son, Rudi, his ex-wife Martha, and ex-brother in law, Richard, he had no hope of leaving Germany. His fate would only become more tragic.

For Uncle Richard, once he received the needed affidavit and the American visa, his perspective on his future underwent a radical change. He knew the United States was a true democratic republic, with laws that enshrined rights that no longer existed in Germany. He knew he must learn a completely new language. He knew he would have to completely start his career over at age 40. He knew that other family members needed to get out of Germany to America, and he was dedicated to finding a way to help them once he settled in New York. He was very worried about two of his siblings, Heinrich and Thekla. He did not know that the United States would give him another chance and an unexpected way to oppose the Nazis.

1. Thalmann and Feinermann, p 26
2. Ibidem
3. Ibidem
4. Idem, p 27
5. Idem, p 33
6. Idem, p 40
7. Idem, p 42
8. Idem, p 57
9. Idem, p 58
10. Cologne During National Socialism, p 189
11. Bracher, p 367
12. Ibidem
13. Craig, p 633
14. Bracher, p 368
15. Idem, p 367

8

FAREWELL, DEAR RICHARD

When I was a little boy living in West Virginia, Dad would call Uncle Richard on February 22, both his and George Washington's birthday. He would hand me the phone so I could wish him a happy birthday. My uncle would greet me saying, "Hello, George Vashington shpeaking." I laughed at his imitation of Washington. As a child, I did not realize why it was part of his American pride. He loved and admired the United States from the moment he arrived, but his dedication deepened from experiencing life here. America grew from just a place for safety to his place of hope for much of the family. It was the country with the civic values Germany surrendered to Nazism.

As Uncle Richard and his family entered 1939, their life felt like it was collapsing due to the raging Nazi oppression. A month felt like a year. Family in the United States provided the required affidavits so the visas could be issued. They were booked to leave on an American ship, the SS Manhattan, on May 15 from Hamburg. But a difficulty arose. The American consulate officials in Stuttgart found some information lacking from Nana's application. Only Uncle Richard received his visa. Now the issue was whether he should proceed to New York without his sister and nephew, as they had to rebook their boarding on the SS Manhattan to August 28 from Hamburg. In an emotional family discussion, it was decided that Uncle Richard would proceed to America. That way, he could find a job and rent an apartment, thus laying the groundwork for their new life away from Germany. Nana and Dad were nervous that war might erupt any time, preventing them from escaping Germany.

On May 11, 1939, a group of Uncle Richard's close friends and family gathered in a former Rhineland lodge to celebrate his departure to live in freedom in America. One of his closest friends, Julius Rutkowsky, wrote and recited this poem about Uncle Richard (translated from German). It represented the feelings of Uncle Richard's family and friends.

There is a well known city,
a cathedral city
on the bank of the Rhine,
where we enjoyed living, joking,
and laughing at *Karneval* time
where we were never plagued
with torment before,
Cologne on the Rhine.
There was a house in this city,
filled with beds and quilts,
tidy and neatly arranged,
The house stood on Marsilstein,
the man who lived there,
everybody loved him so much
–Richard Stern.
You frequently saw him standing,
quite unspoiled,
leaning comfortably against the front door,
He always reflected
a peaceful smile on his mouth.
There he stood free from sorrow,

but now, no more.
Daily life as it used to be,
changed to unbearable to him over time.
He moved the store upstairs,
from the ground floor to the first floor,
And the store below was rented,
as the time required.
He had no cause to complain,
since his life he could still sustain.
But then approached
the black 10th of November,
With horror that we remember.
His feelings were trashed
by the way his store was smashed.
Now Richard thought,
like all others wanted to be probable,
To emigrate as soon as possible.
Fortunately, having a feeling in advance,
in Stuttgart with his sister he did register,
He leaves us now,
but here he must leave his sister.
That however, is no cause to suffer,
because she will follow him
in the near future.
Her affidavit was not in order so here for a while she must stay,
But that time will finally pass away.
Now comes the
"Manhattan by desire,
that captures our Richard,
Takes him away from Germany,
carries him to the United States,
We just must put up with being separated.
In these bad times
one soon suffers bankruptcy,
For you,
may God be one of deep heartfelt mercy,

And from the bottom of our hearts
we all wish you quite soon,
A good, beautiful and large earnings.
Though we wept
through separation and letting go,
No matter how
the changing times are changing,
Everyone likes to think
of the beautiful hours that have connected
you often to friends.
Farewell, dear Richard,
we will never forget you.

Julius Rutkowsky was an actor and a stage manager at the Jewish Rhein-Ruhr Kulturbund theater. After the war began, he was deported from Cologne to Izbica, Poland. In 1942, he was sent to the Majdanek concentration camp, where he was murdered.

On May 14, the day before boarding the SS Manhattan, Richard's sister Thekla also gave him a poem. It expressed how she expected to join him in the United States in 1940. Thekla pointed out Uncle Richard would be the fourth family member in the United States, following their sister Hilda, her husband Ludwig, and their daughter Lee. She described how his life had been destroyed in Cologne. Thekla jokingly suggested that for a first job, he should become a *zappes*, which is Cologne dialect for a beer tapper, warning him not to pour too much behind his own tie. She also advised him to start seeing and dating women as part of building a new life in "the land of opportunity." Her poem ended by telling him not to lose his sense of humor.

Uncle Richard landed in New York on May 24, 1939. Seeing the Statue of Liberty made a deep impression on him, representing the life he hoped to be entering. He was now 40 years old, middle-aged, no longer youthful. Unlike most immigrants from Germany, Uncle Richard had three hundred marks with him instead of 10. This helped him to get settled in New York. For a short time, he lived with his sister Hilda and her husband until he got his first job as a dishwasher in restaurants, working as many hours as possible, earning enough to rent an apartment in Corona, Queens. Hardly knowing a word of English when boarding the SS Manhattan, Uncle Richard attended constant evening classes that did not overlap with work. He focused on getting life ready for his sister and nephew when, hopefully, they would arrive in early September. Because of the need for new education, plus the search for better level jobs, the restart of his life felt like it was once again developing after childhood.

Meanwhile, Dad and Nana struggled to stay safe and acquire enough food in Cologne. They had little money outside of what Dad earned in cash through his job for the non-Jewish upholstery frame producer arranged by Uncle Richard. He also made a little money repairing furniture for some Jewish families. In July 1939, Dad and Nana were called to the American consulate in Stuttgart to finally get their visas. Their visa exam date was on Dad's 16th birthday, July 11. The examination session was nerve-wracking, but they passed all aspects with no further problems. They were on schedule to board the SS Manhattan in Hamburg on what was originally scheduled for August 28.

As July turned to August, Dad felt increased tension over the probability of war erupting with Poland before he and his mom could leave Germany. He knew this was likely once the Molotov-Ribbentrop pact, an agreement between Germany and the Soviet Union to divide Poland, was signed on August 23. He knew the SS Manhattan would be boarding in Le Havre, France. When Dad told his mom they should not go to Hamburg for the boat because of the political instability, she countered that they had passports, visas, and tickets, so there was no problem. For a whole day, he pestered her about the change, emphasizing he could travel to France by himself since he had his own passport. Dad insisted his mom would have to go to Hamburg alone. Finally, she gave in, and they got transit visas for Belgium and France within one day.

Dad and Nana got on a morning train for Paris sometime before August 26. At Aachen, the German side of the border with Belgium, Nazi soldiers forced every passenger off the train. Both males and females were stripped and searched. Dad and his mom were let go and only had the equivalent of eight dollars between them. The stops at the Belgian and French sides of the borders were much calmer, so they already felt the relief of leaving Germany after just a few hours of traveling. Later that day, during the afternoon, they arrived in Paris. The next morning Dad found their way to the United States Lines office.

They showed a window clerk their tickets. The clerk spoke German and asked Dad, "What are you doing here? You were supposed to board the ship in Hamburg." Dad replied, "We thought it was too politically unstable and we should try to board the ship in Le Havre." The clerk responded, "Very clever, young man. We just got a wire canceling the stop of the ship in Hamburg." He continued that the SS Manhattan would only stop in Le Havre, Southampton, England, and then go right to New York. If Dad and Nana had actually gone to Hamburg, they would have waited for a ship that would never have shown up. The clerk told them to take the next train to Le Havre, where they should wait for boarding.

They went to the train station, Gare du Nord, and caught the next Le Havre train. They had to spend two days just waiting for the SS Manhattan. Having almost no money to spend, they stayed in a flophouse and ate as little, simple food as possible. Finally, on August 30, they were able to board the ship. There were so many passengers trying to leave Europe, they ended up having to share their cabin with numerous others. The SS Manhattan sailed to Southampton, leaving there August 31. World War II began on September 1, 1939, as Germany invaded Poland. Dad and Nana had escaped Europe with only one day to spare. On September 7, the liner arrived in New York. Their lives as refugees now began as they reunited with Uncle Richard, also staying with Hilda and Ludwig Walker.

A couple of days after arriving, Dad wanted to go to a liberal synagogue like the Roonstrasse to thank God for his and Nana's safe arrival in New York. He was recommended to pray at Temple Emanuel in Manhattan. He arrived there, looked around for a yarmulke, but could not find one, as Emanuel was a classic

American Reform temple, far less traditional than the liberal synagogues in Germany. So Dad kept his cap on while sitting down in the sanctuary. An usher came up to him and told him, in German, to remove his cap. Dad responded, "Oh, I thought this was a synagogue," and got up to leave. The usher told him it was a synagogue. That was one of the first interesting differences he experienced between the United States and Germany.

By the end of 1939, Uncle Richard, Dad, and Nana were living together in their own apartment in Corona, Queens. Uncle Richard was still working in restaurants as either a busboy or a dishwasher. Nana was a maid for a well-to-do household. Dad enrolled in Murray Hill High School in New York, focusing on learning English as well as continuing woodwork training. He felt accepted by his teachers and fellow students, getting an immediate positive feeling about living in America. In a letter to a cousin, Uncle Richard wrote that a family of three needed a minimum income of twenty dollars a week to live. While he would try to advance to a better job, they were earning what was needed. Unlike so many relatives still in Germany, Uncle Richard felt life was uncomplicated, even if not rewarding. He sensed goodness in the United States. He hoped others in his family would be able to come and experience the same sense of freedom, writing that in letters to numerous family members.

On the morning of November 10, 1938, while the pogrom of *Kristallnacht* continued, Uncle Richard's brother-in-law, Heinz Flogerhover, dealt with Nazi SAs who came into his print shop next door to Uncle Richard's store, claiming his was also a Jewish business. Heinz denied that, as he was Catholic, yet the Nazis shouted it was on their list of Jewish shops. They ended up smashing the windows but not doing any other damage. The next day, Heinz took his two daughters, Ruth and Ellen, on a walk down to the Rhine River, throwing a service revolver into the water. This was the first in a series of decisions he made with his wife, Uncle

Richard's sister Thekla, about what the family should do. Their daughter, Ruth, was old enough to get a job, so they arranged for her to become a nanny for a family in England. She left in May 1939. Their younger daughter, Ellen, was 13, and they wanted to get her out of Germany as well.

Heinz and Thekla contacted smugglers who could be paid to take people across the border to Belgium. It took three attempts, but she made it to Brussels in the late summer of 1939. Her parents then tried a few times to cross the border in the same manner, even after Belgium passed a law saying that someone crossing the border from Germany had to go to jail for a while. Thekla and Heinz decided jail in Belgium was better than living in Germany. They succeeded in crossing in the fall of 1939. Uncle Richard noted in a letter written April 15, 1940, to other cousins that Thekla and Heinz were in prison for over six weeks but were finally living in Chateau Marneffe, Belgium, in an internment camp. He was hoping to get all the Flogerhover family over to America as soon as possible. Along with Nana, he was talking to the cousin who organized their affidavits to do it for the Flogerhovers.

On May 10, 1940, Germany invaded Belgium. The camp holding the Flogerhovers and other refugees closed down and told them to walk toward France. But the German army moved so fast, it got in front of the group, forcing them to turn toward Brussels. It took weeks to get there. For a while, they stayed at a farm in a pigsty. Not identified as Jews, the Flogerhovers, along with numerous refugees, were picked up by German soldiers heading to Brussels. They did not speak to the soldiers, who were trying to create a positive impression of their occupation to the Belgian population. Finally, with the help of the Belgian Red Cross, the Flogerhovers made it to Brussels, finding family that had moved there a number of years earlier. They owned an empty house and allowed the Flogerhovers to live there. This would turn out to be only temporary safety. Uncle Richard was hoping they had escaped but was starting to worry because he did not hear much from them.

On February 22, 1939, Uncle Richard's brother Heinrich also fled to Brussels. This seemed to be a common place to flee for

German-Jewish war veterans from World War I. His wife, Frieda, and twelve-year-old daughter, Elisa, joined him three days later. On March 1, 1940, a little more than two months before Germany invaded France, Heinrich's German citizenship was officially ended. They got an apartment in Brussels, staying safe until May 9, 1941, when Heinrich was arrested on the street and sent with many other Jews to St. Cyprien in France, close to the border with Spain. His wife and daughter were not arrested and were able to stay in Belgium. According to a letter written on November 5, Heinrich was taken to "the grotto of St. Cyprien." He reported to his family in New York that his money and valuables had been confiscated by Belgians while he was temporarily in Ettelbruck, Luxemburg. By October 30, he was imprisoned in a detainment camp in Gurs, France. He closed the letter to his siblings in New York, asking them to send him some money.

The last words anyone got from Heinrich were in a letter to his wife and daughter written on July 19, 1942. By that time, he had not received any communication from his family in New York for a year. He had been struggling with his health but stated he had been doing better. His daughter, now 16 years old, had apparently written a great letter that cheered him up. He expressed his sadness over the death of his uncle, Leopold Stern, who died in a hospital from an illness on March 31, 1942. Shortly after this letter, Heinrich was taken to Drancy, a deportation point. On August 10, 1942, he was sent to the concentration camp at Auschwitz. At this point, Uncle Richard knew his brother was taken to the detainment camp in Gurs but did not learn he was sent to Auschwitz for over a year, late in 1943. Even then, he did not know the level of genocide occurring there. Neither did he know, in 1942, about the death of his Uncle Leopold.

Dad's longest childhood friend, Lou Gruenebaum, made it to America in an unusual circumstance. In June of 1938, his father was taken by the Nazis to the concentration camp of Sachsenhausen. He was beaten and forced to give away his business. He came home to Cologne on August 8, 1938, and realized he had to immediately leave Germany. Lou's dad got a visa for Mexico and left on August

27, and upon arriving in Mexico 15 days later, he had to bribe the Mexican authorities to allow him into the country. Lou continued to live in Germany just with his twin sister and their mother, as their mother thought that the persecutions against the Jews would blow over. *Kristallnacht* proved how she was entirely wrong. By January of 1940, Lou and his sister received visas to the United States. Their mom still refused to go with them. They arrived in New York on February 15, 1940, where relatives picked up Lou and his sister to go live in Pittsburgh with them. Finally, their mother applied for a visa to Mexico and received it just before she would have been sent to a concentration camp. She arrived safely to be with her husband.

After Dad had the one memorable experience of being with his biological father, Walter Romberg, when he got his signature on the emigration paperwork, he began to wonder who Walter really was. He wondered if the voices he'd heard in the apartment actually belonged to his children. He kept hearing from his mother, Uncle Richard, and a number of other Stern family members that his father was awful. However, after he settled in New York, his Uncle Ludwig, married to Uncle Richard's sister Hilda, quietly told Dad that Walter was really not that terrible. Dad, for much of his life, kept trying to find information about Walter.

When I lived in Israel for a year, from 1996 to 1997, Dad asked me to research in various museums that had information on German Jews to see what I could find. I had no success. When Dad was visiting friends in Cologne in 1999, one had good connections with the German government and found he had four half-siblings fathered by Walter Romberg. The oldest, Charlotte, and Dad became close for the last nine years of his life. I met her in 2013 and learned the fate of Walter Romberg, my grandfather.

His apartment until 1937 was decent. Afterward, they had to constantly change apartments, living in four more over the next five years, each one getting worse. Instead of a bathroom within their apartment, they had to share toilets at the staircase with other families in the building. Walter loved music and loved to read, in particular books by Heinrich Heine, which were illegal under Nazi rule. He hid them deep in a clothes closet. Walter mocked Nazi leaders. Here was his joke about Hermann Goering, "The more the decoration, the more the decoration. The fatter this person gets."

Once, Walter was required to do forced work for the Nazi government for pay that was next to nothing. Yet, he tried to provide things for his children. Charlotte wanted a doll pram, so he found one from friends. But Charlotte thought it was so old fashioned she was embarrassed to get it. On their way home from picking it up, they stopped to get lemonade at a kiosk, leaving it at the side to see if anyone would take it while they were drinking. No one did, so they brought it home, and those who saw the pram laughed at it. On a more serious level, Walter worried about food for his family. He would purposely bring back some of the food his wife gave him to eat at work. He cut it into small sections for his children and called it "rabbit food." While the children played and ate, Walter would hug each of them, in the end embracing them all together.

Most significant about Walter, however, was how he tried to help Jewish families in different ways from 1938 onward. For those who were trying to leave, he knew how to fill out forms for the different bureaucracies. On the second floor of the building where Walter's family lived in 1941, there was a Jewish family with twin girls the same age as Charlotte, who became her friends. While Jewish families were being deported to concentration camps, Walter helped them take their suitcases with a handcart he owned. For those taken to deportation camps right near Cologne, he would walk with them. The family with Charlotte's friends was deported at first to Minsk, then put on a truck they were told was taking them to a work place. However, Charlotte learned years later that the truck was a traveling gas chamber that murdered the family. While in many ways he was so different than Uncle Richard, Walter Romberg also showed love for family and caring for people in need. Perhaps the biggest difference was the end of his life being much more tragic.

Walter's forced job was changed to practically slave labor in a toxic chemical factory. On Sunday, August 2, 1942, Walter was at home, lying ill in bed. Charlotte, at 10 years old, was in the kitchen cooking with her mother. Walter came in, started to sob, collapsed, then died from the poisonous chemicals he had been exposed to in the factory. As Walter's body was being taken out of the apartment building for the funeral, Charlotte stood on the street crying. A girl from a Nazi family that lived in the building said to her, "Why are you crying? That's just a Jew."

Uncle Richard's life in the United States was gaining stability as 1940 began, but he could not abandon his concerns for family members still trapped in Germany. He knew his brother Heinrich, Heinrich's wife Frieda, and their daughter Elisa were stuck in Brussels as well as his sister Thekla, husband Heinz and daughter Ellen. Thekla's daughter Ruth was working in England as a nanny. Uncle Richard was trying to save twelve hundred dollars to help the Flogerhovers get to America. However, it was the fate and problems of his cousin, Henni Katz, her husband Carl, and their son Michael, that forced him to take on additional responsibility.

Carl Katz sold his and Henni's home in 1937, then his butcher business in February of 1938. Despite the German oppression of Jews earning profit, the sales did provide some financial security. In January 1938, their son Helmut, who made it safely to South Africa, got married and the Katz family celebrated in their Cologne apartment. Shortly after, their life began to get seriously worse. Their son Michael, who had been working in the family's shop, but now was forbidden to continue, was forced into road-building work by the German government. As 1938 continued, some relatives in the large Katz family made plans to leave Germany. Some still felt the oppression by the Nazi government would calm down at some point and did not want to leave. What made emigrating more difficult for German Jews was a law instated October 5, 1938, which required their passports to be stamped with a large "J" to indicate they were Jewish. Michael had applied to follow his brother Helmut to South Africa, but his application was rejected. *Kristallnacht* changed their recognition of reality.

Carl had been in bad health when the pogrom happened on November 9 and 10, 1938. When arrested by the Gestapo, their treatment of him made it worse. They interrogated Carl by forcing him to sit on a stool, exhausting him, and he kept falling off. The Gestapo released Carl, and in early 1939, he and Henni again changed apartments. The Nazis forced the Katz family to sell all of their real estate and to live only in a rented apartment. In April, Jews lost any legal protection as either tenants or landlords. Michael was now making a plan to leave Germany, go to his Uncle Ludwig Katz in Amsterdam, Netherlands, from there continue over to England, and then immigrate to the United States. Through 1939, Henni and Carl were looking for a way to follow their son to England and hopefully join him in America.

While dancing in "Café Silberbach," one of the only places in Cologne where Jews were still allowed, Michael met and fell in love with Ilse Frank. The two of them were planning to meet in Amsterdam and continue together to England. Michael's train reservation was set for August 14, 1939. Just before he left, his parents held a farewell gathering for him attended by the Flogerhovers, Thekla, Heinz, and Ellen, as well as Nana and Dad. Carl took his son to the train and blessed him as he said goodbye. Henni stayed at home, crying. Michael arrived at his Uncle Ludwig's house in Amsterdam, but Ilse was delayed and could not join him in time to go to England.

Michael arrived in England on August 22. He settled in London and had a hard time adjusting to the huge metropolis. Ilse made it directly to London shortly after Michael, but she moved to Bristol to take a job with a nursing home. She and Michael shared each other's worries in letters. As Great Britain entered World War II at the beginning of September, Michael and Ilse were both considered "hostile foreigners." He struggled, finding a short-term job, as the longer-term plan included his parents meeting him in London by the end of September. It never happened. Uncle Ludwig's British business partner became a guarantor for Michael, pledging he would not need any government financial aid. Later that fall, Michael finally got a butcher job in London but decided to move to Bristol to be with Ilse, finding a job there.

Once Germany and Great Britain were officially at war after September 1, 1939, it was impossible for Henni and Carl Katz, who were stuck in Cologne, to get letters to their sons, one in South Africa the other in England. Uncle Richard stepped in, since the United States was not yet in the war, receiving the letters from either side of the Katz family in New York, often rewriting them on American letterhead, then sending them in a new envelope with the New York return address to either England, South Africa, or Cologne. He wrote his own letters to each Katz family member, working with them to stay in contact as well as trying to find a way to get them to the United States.

In late October 1939, Michael wrote to his family that he and Ilse were getting engaged. His parents were not in favor of them getting married, believing he was too young and too early in his attempt to settle in England to enter a serious relationship. Carl and Henni's hope to get to England by the end of September had disappeared, yet Carl wrote a series of arguments to his son against his engagement to Ilse, saying he should focus on the responsibility of helping his parents in their attempt to emigrate from Germany. Carl added that engagement to Ilse would destroy Michael's hope for a better future. Carl and Henni also disapproved of Ilse because her family was not butchers, so she had no experience being a family member in that kind of work. This rejection felt tragic to Michael and Ilse, but an even deeper tragedy occurred in mid-December of 1939, when Ilse's mother, still in Germany, committed suicide.

In a letter written to Michael and Ilse on April 15, 1940, Uncle Richard expressed a completely different viewpoint about their marriage, in addition to his condolences to Ilse over the death of her mother. He noted that the culture regarding personal relationships was much different than before 1935, in which so many anti-Jewish laws were passed, and 1938 in which the awful *Kristallnacht* happened. He congratulated them on their engagement, saying that each person "is the architect of his own fortune." He told them he had written to Michael's parents that they should give up their outdated point of view. Uncle Richard assured them their differences with Michael's parents would get resolved.

In January of 1940, Henni and Carl's financial situation was becoming more precarious. They were still hoping to find a way to get to the United States and perhaps continue traveling to be with their son Helmut in South Africa. On February 17, they received a letter from the American consulate in Stuttgart, stating they needed an affidavit from someone living in America. They mailed the document to Ludwig in Amsterdam for him to forward to someone in New York to provide that affidavit. Meanwhile, Michael was trying to organize his and Ilse's immigration to the United States and was thinking it would be easier if they went ahead and got married. Carl and Henni still opposed their marriage, wanting him to help take care of their immigration, but their lives continued to fall apart. Henni had been suffering some heart problems.

When it was clear there could be no preventing Michael and Ilse from getting married, Carl wrote a letter dated April 1 giving them a blessing. It was an emotionally difficult move for him. On April 10, Carl suffered a stomach ache, was placed in the Jewish hospital, and died on April 18, 1940. Henni's situation, like all Western European Jews, declined further on May 10, 1940, when Germany launched the invasion that conquered Belgium, the Netherlands, and France. She could no longer communicate directly with Michael or Helmut. Ludwig Katz in Amsterdam could not communicate for her either, as his own life was now in danger. It was on May 14 that Uncle Richard responded to his cousin Henni assuring her that he would take care of sending her family's communications to each other. It became the only way that Henni could stay in contact with her sons.

In late April of 1940, Uncle Richard came down with a bad case of tonsillitis and was stuck in bed for three weeks, missing work. Apparently, this was a common illness among new immigrants. His letter to Henni offering to take care of family communications occurred while he was sick. He went back to work as a busboy on May 23. In a letter to Michael Katz written on May 22 in which he shared this news, he first wrote his condolence over the death of Michael's father, Carl. Uncle Richard was only 28 years old when he lost his father, Markus, and he told Michael, "Everybody has such moments, but they make you even stronger in the struggle for life." He told Michael about hearing other family losses shortly after Carl's death. With Nazi Germany's conquest of France, Belgium, and the Netherlands, threats to the Jewish population increased. He was quite worried about his brother Heinrich, his sister Thekla and their families – all in Belgium.

His sickness had no doubt delayed the pursuit of a better job, but in December of 1940, Uncle Richard finally found one, working for Charles Textile Company, a textile printing business. In a letter to Michael Katz from January 17, 1941, he said this comically about his job change, "My income has increased, and the foundation for my first million (dollars) is laid." Since his niece Ruth was also living in England, he asked Michael to give her financial aid in getting to the United States, and Uncle Richard would pay him back. He also told a story about a mutual family friend, Manfred Cohen, who also immigrated to America. Cohen had joined the U.S. Army to serve as a soldier for a year. This was months before the United States entered the war. A couple of months later, he wrote a humorous bit on Cohen, saying he was already on his second vacation from the army and he would soon become a general since the army needed one.

Throughout his letters to Michael Katz, Uncle Richard continuously pushed why he and Ilse should immigrate to the United States. In one letter, he wrote, "This country is amazing; when you get here, you will understand what I meant." He was thrilled that his birthday was a national holiday, happily noting that February 22 was also George Washington's birthday. In another letter, Uncle Richard stated, "we are happy and grateful to live in this free country." In more sad news that Uncle Richard learned by March of 1941, there were 15 other family members, besides his brother Heinrich, in the Gurs detainment camp.

By August of 1941, Uncle Richard was a union member, which improved his ability to work for a higher-paying company. He got a job at Gselle Textile Printing Corp., earning another six to eight dollars per week. This had him in the range of over 40 per week on a consistent basis. His employer got so busy in the fall that he worked for twelve hours per day, taking home some projects at night and supervising work done by four to six others on his own. This pushed his income to a high point of 55 dollars per week. He believed his English was still insufficient and wrote how a friend of his said that properly learning English would take as long as becoming a millionaire. At this point, he was also very proud of Dad, who, only one year out of high school, was already working as a skilled cabinetmaker earning 26 dollars a week.

Cousin Henni sent Uncle Richard a letter in mid-June of 1940 after he volunteered to control the communication between her and her sons, Helmut and Michael. She asked him to help them by keeping them informed as well as trying to get Michael and his new wife, Ilse, to America. She told him about Martha de Strelecky's financial ability to help get Katz family members out of Germany, the key piece being affidavits committing money to family immigrants. Henni hoped that Michael and Ilse were coming to America and wondered if they would be moving in with Uncle Richard. What he desperately wanted was to get Henni out of Germany, preferably to the United States. She had said she was stuck in Cologne and would do whatever she could to stay strong but deeply desired to see her children once again.

So much of his non-working time was engaged in trying to figure a way to get family to America, whether Henni, the Flogerhovers, and possibly even Heinrich, Frieda, and Elisa. Despite the continuous increase in weekly earnings, it was impossible for Uncle Richard to have enough money to cover more than the Flogerhover family's travel costs, which he figured would be 1,200 dollars. Dealing with life had been so much more complicated through the war's intensification in May 1940, a number of family members' deaths, the increasingly violent persecution of European Jews, and the decreasing availability of transportation out of Europe. Yet, Uncle Richard expressed optimism to Michael in his May 22, 1940 letter. "Much has changed, but that is not a reason for despair, we have to stay calm and one must keep one's nerves there." Living in the United States inspired Uncle Richard to once again find a way to stand up against the Nazis.

In March of 1941, Uncle Richard was still trying to get an affidavit for Henni. He visited a Katz family relative, Solomon Guggenheimer, but he was not allowed to issue any more affidavits because he had issued so many for closer relatives. He also noted how tied up Martha de Strelecky was. She had done the same as Guggenheimer. Uncle Richard grew frustrated as he was barely able to raise enough for his own sister, Thekla, Heinz, and Ellen. He wrote in a letter to Michael on March 23 that he hoped to get Helmut to cover Henni's travel cost. He noted how booked ship cabins were, filled until June. He asked Michael to contact his brother. Despite his frustration, Uncle Richard was still able to joke, telling Michael to give some sausage to his niece Ruth in order to keep her chubby.

In many of the letters Uncle Richard sent to Michael, he would either send a full letter to Thekla's daughter Ruth or include a short note on the letter to Michael. During the first half of 1941, he received fairly constant letters from Thekla, so he would let Ruth know how her parents were doing since her letters from England could not be delivered to them in Belgium. Uncle Richard encouraged Ruth to send letters for her parents to him, as he could forward them to Belgium. He also urged her to immigrate to the United States. Ruth could be hard to deal with, so Uncle Richard often asked Michael to check on her and see how she was doing. He wrote to Michael that while Ruth had a difficult personality, she truly had a "good and honest character." In another letter, he pointed out how experiencing difficult times causes young people to mature.

Serious changes were occurring in the summer of 1941. Uncle Richard noticed that Henni's writing style had changed. He knew the predicament was getting worse—not just for Henni, but for all

German Jews. He was still hoping that Martha de Strelecky might be able to provide the affidavit for Henni. Her son Helmut had written him that because of the war, he could not send any money to Henni in Cologne. With a letter sent to Michael on August 4, Uncle Richard included letterheads with his address so that any letter Michael wrote to his mother would appear it was from New York, not England. He instructed him to keep the letter to one page and not to use any words that implied he was not in Uncle Richard's neighborhood. Uncle Richard was also concerned that the change in US immigration regulations would result in visa applications being postponed until after the war.

By the fall of 1941, Cologne's Jews faced deteriorating conditions. From September onward, all Jews were forced to wear badges with yellow Jewish stars.[1] They were forced to live in jammed apartment "ghettos." Uncle Richard learned from new Jewish immigrants from Cologne about how they had to give their furnished apartments to Aryans and were forced to live in overcrowded apartments. Henni, while able to stay in her apartment, had four or five people forced to live with her. Jews pushed out of their apartments had to give away their furniture. The RAF (Great Britain's air force) had started some bombing of Cologne, but Henni had not suffered from that. It was now impossible for anyone to leave Germany.

By November of 1941, deportations to ghettos and concentration camps were underway in Cologne.[2] Late in the fall, Uncle Richard and Martha de Strelecki agreed to process a Cuban visa for Henni. It cost 1,200 dollars. Uncle Richard and Nana gave one hundred dollars, and a number of Katz family members contributed as well. Uncle Richard sent fabricated telegrams to Cologne stating he was about to acquire the Cuban visa. This was his attempt to delay Henni's possible deportation, which he learned was frequently happening from new Jewish immigrants to the United States. Even at the end of December, Uncle Richard was still hoping to find a way to save Henni. The last letter he received from her was written on October 30, 1941. The last letter anyone in the Katz family received from her was dated November 20, 1941. Uncle Richard had received a cable from her via Amsterdam on November 22 and sent a telegram to Michael Katz on December 4, making him believe she had not yet been deported as all telegram communication with Henni had gone in and out of Amsterdam. Sometime in early December, Henni was deported by train to the Riga ghetto in Latvia. She became missing and was officially declared dead after the war

In January of 1942, Uncle Richard had no idea where Henni was. He was no longer receiving communication from the Flogerhovers in Belgium. He had heard nothing more about his brother Heinrich, his wife Frieda, or their daughter. He despised what Germany had become. He referred in family letters to the "Nazi dogs" having to get their deserved punishment. In a letter to Michael and Ilse written January 25, 1942, he shared his desire to serve in the American army to beat the Nazis. He said he would be registered by February 16 and prayed he would be drafted by February 17. He wrote about his anger and how fighting the Nazis would give him great satisfaction.

Uncle Richard had grown to love America. The United States stood for all the liberties he had been denied by the fall of the Weimar Republic and the rise of the Third Reich. For the rest of his life, he would be totally committed to the United States. The United States declared war on Japan on December 8, 1941, the day after the attack on Pearl Harbor. On December 11, 1941, Germany declared war on the United States. Uncle Richard, at 42 years old, could have lived a good, safe life, earning more money now that he was settled in New York and advancing to a better job. That was not his destiny.

He was emotionally frustrated from the increasing lack of knowledge on the fates of his relatives, now including his brother Heinrich and his family, his sister Thekla and her family, plus his cousin Henni. In his heart and in his mind, he was motivated to fight against Nazi Germany and find a way to search for his family. Once America was officially in World War II, metal was collected from any citizen who wanted to contribute. This metal could be used to do anything from building boats to bullets. Uncle Richard contributed the Iron Cross he was awarded from Germany during the First World War, hoping it would be made into bullets used to kill the Nazis. This was his first step into the war.

Farewell gathering for Richard Stern (May 11, 1939)

---

1. Cologne During National Socialism, p 191
2. Ibidem

9

THE HAND-PAINTED FLAG

"I want to stay here and shall not go to Europe to fight against any country, because this war is an imperialistic war, and England does not fight for democracy," my dad wrote in a letter to his cousin Michael Katz in England on April 15, 1940, seven months after arriving in the United States. Uncle Richard must have seen what Dad wrote because this letter was enclosed with my uncle's letter to Michael. Dad was only 16 at this point. Expressing this thought must have reinforced Uncle Richard's constant teaching about the necessity to oppose Nazism.

The letters Richard wrote to Dad once he made it into the US Army often stressed the importance of participating in the war against Germany. At the end of his training period, just before being shipped overseas in August 1943, he wrote to Dad,

> "We are all in good spirit and we have been waiting for ten years for the day to come. It is my own will to go to war at forty-four years old. We all hope that the Nazi beasts and their allies will be destroyed. I don't have to remind you because you experienced it yourself. We will never forget the cruelties to our brothers, relatives, and all our friends."

Obviously, Uncle Richard felt Dad needed to be reminded, even though he constantly expressed these feelings from the moment they moved to the United States. Even after Dad joined the US Army, Richard frequently wrote to him about their obligation to participate in the war.

Uncle Richard admitted that in the early 1930s, he had underestimated the effect of the rising Nazi movement. After his protest during the Nazi boycott of Jewish businesses, he became silent, afraid of being arrested once again and sent to a concentration camp. As his business continuously declined, he did not push it openly but hid it more, just focusing on a smaller customer group. He viewed his experiences in the 1930s as a failure, and he hated how he struggled with the change from being a patriotic, heroic German to just a Jewish victim. He felt ashamed that he did not adequately predict the coming loss of civil rights in Germany. Once Uncle Richard fled to America, he began to learn that the ideals he stood for in the doorway of his store on April 1, 1933, could actually exist. Instead of just living safely in the United States, he felt moved to choose once again to find a way of taking a stand against the Nazis.

While Uncle Richard wished to be accepted into the US army by February 17, it was not until September 16, 1942, that he received an official notice of acceptance to the army as an alien in America. On September 22, he was sent an order to report for induction into the army on October 13. He was so excited to be officially inducted he created a special hand-painted American flag to send as a gift to the officer he saw in charge at the induction, Major John Scially. After one week of preparation to report for training, he sent the painted flag along with a letter to Major Scially. He expressed his appreciation of the kindness shown to him, especially as he was a foreigner, and added:

"As a former German soldier I have learned the spirit which conducts this army. It is entirely the opposite of Prussian militarism, with all its brutal chicanery."

He then described how German recruits were treated like dogs serving a master. He pledged to use his experience as a German soldier to help the morale of his future American comrades.

Upon receiving the letter and gift, Major Scially immediately sent him a thank-you letter. He wrote he would always cherish not just the gift, but what Uncle Richard expressed about serving in the German army, and added,

> "You see, Richard, if only some people could realize and appreciate this wonderful land of ours as you do, it would make those people happier. I believe that over there (referring to Germany) a recruit must be just another nothing while here a recruit is a human being with every consideration given him by our great government."

The major's response represented a principle Uncle Richard felt was typical in the United States.

Uncle Richard did not often deliver a speech, but after getting drafted into the American army, he proudly gave one to his co-union members working at Gsell Textile Print Co. Being drafted, he told them, was a huge honor. He shared his experiences with the German army in World War I, then emphasized that battling for democracy as an American soldier was the central purpose in his life. The civil rights he stood up for in Germany as the Weimar Republic fell apart became an inspiration for entering the American army in addition to standing against the oppression of his fellow Jews.

His service actually began on October 27. On the previous day, he had composed a will to his siblings living in New York, describing his wishes if he died in battle in addition to how his assets should be distributed. He began with the hope that Nazi power would be destroyed, and all of the Stern siblings would be able to come together once again. He made it clear that part of the distribution of his assets should include Thekla and Heinrich, who were stuck in countries occupied by Germany. His assets included

10,000 dollars from life insurance, which would all go to Martha (Nana). All the rest, which included war bonds, were to be divided among all the siblings. One of Dad's teachers in Germany, Dr. Kober, had immigrated to New York and was the rabbi of a small German-Jewish congregation. Uncle Richard left his large Kiddush cup plus one hundred dollars to the congregation in honor of *Kaddish* for their parents. He requested that the first male descendant be named after him. Perhaps the most interesting was an appeal to his sisters Martha and Hilda to respect each other more, in particular for Martha to behave more honorably by ignoring the overdramatic issues Hilda would often seem to invent. He felt Martha had to try harder not to react furiously over items she did not like, especially if he was not around to help. To all of the family, he closed with this statement,

"Always stick together like we have done until now. Remember our perfect past, stay healthy, and may you soon start new families. The old comes to an end, the new comes into being."

Uncle Richard typed the will, but at the bottom, handwrote this, "Victory for this beautiful country of U.S.A."

He began his training at Camp Upton on Long Island, New York. The recruits were all shown a movie on venereal disease and then given an intelligence test. In his first letter written to the family from the army, on October 28, he raved about how good the food was at every meal. On November 9, he was sent for his full training, where afterward, there might be some specialty training at Fort McClellan, near Anniston, Alabama. After a meal with 200 fellow soldiers to celebrate Thanksgiving, he mentioned how delicious the turkey was and that he saved half of it for the next day. Uncle Richard also felt he was making good progress in his training to become a soldier. He was assigned to be the leader in a group of four trainees. In early December, a general selected him to speak for the group and Richard was proud to have answered all the questions correctly. His basic training was for six weeks, part of it occurring during Chanukah. He went to a Chanukah party in Anniston thrown for Jewish soldiers. The USO sent Nana a letter describing the party and talked about Uncle Richard being present.

Family would send him packages with all kinds of gifts, including supplies, tobacco, and candy. In a letter written to the family on December 6, 1942, he joked, "Now I have four toothbrushes, including my last one from Cologne. I have enough to last me for 14 years." He had also received enough candy to open his own candy store and asked them to stop sending so much. The reason? He was concerned about them wasting money on him, as he felt the army treated its recruits very well, especially with the food. In another letter, he wrote feeling heavy, as he now weighed 196 pounds. Basic training was done by December 22. He was still waiting to see his permanent military regiment assignment, whether it would take him to Europe against Germany or to the Pacific against Japan. He was one of only 20 soldiers left to be assigned, and he wrote that his regiment would be decided in January.

On July 25, 1942, the 48th Engineer Combat Regiment was officially activated in Camp Gruber, in the Black Hills area of Oklahoma. The first significant number of additional soldiers arrived in October of 1942. The training was more than basic. It included bridge building and repair, weapons maintenance and cleaning, equipment repair, and filling in shell holes. At this point, there were only 140 men in a regiment that would grow to well over a thousand. A few weeks later, over 800 men came from infantry training in Camp Wolters, Texas.[1] In the beginning of January 1943, a bill was passed discharging from the army essential workers over 38 years old who qualified to work in industries that manufactured war goods. This affected the 48th Regiment heavily, with over 400 replacements needed.[2] Most of the new replacements were from New York City, and those included Uncle Richard. He had been offered the chance to leave the army since he was over 38 years old, but he insisted on staying.

In March 1943, the 48th Regiment went to Louisiana for a series of maneuvers. Once there, it was broken apart into two engineering battalions of three companies each. Companies A (Able), B (Baker), and C (Charlie) became the 48th Engineering Battalion of 600 soldiers. Uncle Richard was placed in the Able Company of the 48th. The living conditions for the soldiers while training in Louisiana were miserable. They stayed in pup tents pitched in the middle of a mud and water area.[3] They did a 25-mile hike under intense Louisiana heat. The first five miles were done in an hour, which took energy out of the soldiers, yet they continued the walk throughout the afternoon. All they were fed were lousy sandwiches, plus they ran out of water in their canteens. The next morning, medics treated the injuries caused by the hike. That is when the battalion's new commander, who led them through the first set of key battles, arrived: Major Andrew Goodpaster.[4]

The purpose of this was to get the battalion ready for difficult living situations overseas. It was clear the battalion would be sent overseas, but Uncle Richard did not know whether it would be to Europe or the Pacific. Over the weeks following that awful first hike, the battalion practiced maneuvers, including segments of infantry battle training. They had no idea how valuable that training would turn out to be. These maneuvers also taught them how to keep information from being uncovered by enemies and sharpened their engineering training.

Meanwhile, Dad was inducted into the army on January 11, 1943, beginning at Camp Upton in New York and continuing basic training at Camp Robinson in Arkansas. When that was completed, he was transferred to the Desert Training Center in western Arizona. In a situation similar to Uncle Richard, his second stage of training felt like it was eroding his strength. He wrote about this to Uncle Richard on May 3. Uncle Richard wrote back to him on May 9, saying he understood how Dad felt, but to know it would pass, and he would end up feeling stronger, becoming used to that style of living after two weeks. He then described his six weeks of living in a pup tent. Afterward, the battalion was moved into larger tents that held five or six people. Richard commented how after living in the pup tents, the bigger tents felt like hotels, adding, "especially, as we have the chance of taking a shower." Uncle Richard was surprised that Dad had moved so quickly to a specific unit. He told him to expect his overseas assignment sometime after June 20. He wondered where his unit would be sent, Africa possibly, or "beautiful" Italy perhaps?

Uncle Richard then wanted to teach Dad another lesson. He wrote about seven people just in Able Company who were in the hospital suffering from gonorrhea from being less than cautious in their sexual relations. He warned Dad to be careful. This was the letter where he described Walter Romberg's unsteady life, which he felt was based on the way he approached sex. He then told Dad this was the basis for his mom's physical infection, which also infected her thinking. This was the first time Dad had learned the reason behind Mom's physical and psychological problems. Most important to Uncle Richard was to keep his knowledge of this a secret, stressing that Dad should not discuss it even with Aunt Hilda, Aunt Thekla, or especially with his mom.

Dad's outlook on participating in the war in Europe had completely changed from when he was finishing high school. Like Uncle Richard, he wanted to go against the Nazis in Europe, so toward the end of August, when he learned his division would be sent to the Pacific, he used his flat feet as a health reason to be discharged from the army. He was honorably discharged on September 25, 1943. Even at the end of May, Uncle Richard had encouraged Dad to use his flat feet to get discharged from the infantry and suggested he then volunteer for an engineering battalion. He stressed that an engineering battalion could do so much work and related how he had just learned how to do chemical testing. He thought Dad would feel fulfilled through engineering work.

It was clear to them that Nana was upset about her two closest family members serving in the army. She was affected physically and mentally by the fear of losing them both. This was part of their letter-based discussion in August 1943. Dad praised Uncle Richard's decision to be in the American army: "I think you are right; in fact you can't be wrong. Fighting these Nazi bastards is the most important part of our life." Later in the fall, Dad applied to go back into the army; he wanted to fight the Germans, not the Japanese. He was working in carpentry while waiting to be readmitted.

The 48th Engineer's Battalion boarded a train on August 10, 1943, not knowing whether they would be taken to the East Coast or West Coast, which would indicate if they were going to be facing the Germans or the Japanese. On August 12, they arrived at Camp Myles Standish, near Taunton, Massachusetts, not far from Boston. In his August 18 letter to Dad, Uncle Richard said he was not allowed to write his actual location; however, he finally knew they would be sent overseas against Germany. He just did not know when they would actually leave.

Uncle Richard's reflections on why he felt it so necessary to be in the US Army at 45 years old was the centerpiece of his August 18 letter. He discussed their sadness over the cruelty he and Dad witnessed not only on themselves but their family and friends. The current situation of Jews in Germany he called the most egregious in the past 1,000 years of German-Jewish history:

"If a dog gets abused, you would be able to criminally charge somebody for cruelty to an animal. Nowadays, everyone can do everything to a Jew, whatever they want to without getting prosecuted by a German court. I hope that a higher justice will prosecute those responsible."

On August 20, the 48th Engineering Battalion got on a train to New York Harbor, where they boarded the USS Edmund B. Alexander, a troop ship that was part of a large convoy surrounded by Navy ships protecting them from German submarines. Richard had seen the Statue of Liberty for the first time on May 24, 1939, while arriving in New York from the ship he sailed on to escape Nazi Germany. A little over four years later, he saw it from a boat taking him back to oppose the Nazis once again. It represented his emotions over living in a country that enjoyed the freedoms he was denied in Germany.

After two weeks at sea, the convoy passed Gibraltar. From being in the Mediterranean, Uncle Richard knew he would end up either in Africa or Sicily. On the morning of September 2, the ship anchored at a harbor in Algeria. The 48th Battalion disembarked, boarded trucks, and traveled to the city of Oran. A camp was set up for them just outside of Oran so that the troops could explore the city a bit. My uncle found this area of Africa to be beautiful and thought Oran was a lovely city. He explored a synagogue he felt was excellent, especially since the High Holidays were only a few weeks away. On September 11, the battalion truck convoyed to St. Dennis du Sig, not far from Oran, where a camp for deeper campaign training was set up.[5] The 48th then had its first campaign, which was against thousands upon thousands of squeamish bugs that invaded the tents of the battalion. They built wooden floors in the tents and dug trenches filled with oil and water around the camp, but they kept coming. The engineer soldiers burned them, sprayed them, and gassed them, but the bugs still came.[6] As the author of *We the 48th* wrote,

"The 48th was outsmarted, outflanked, and outmaneuvered. We went down in defeat and let the bugs crawl where they would."[7]

During the time at St. Dennis du Sig, the battalion trained hard on building, fixing, and tearing down bridges, along with how to handle minefields. Added to the technical training were long hikes and exhausting physical exercises. Uncle Richard never complained about any of this; his letters kept checking on the family's well-being—particularly Nana's health. In a letter to Nana and the family on October 4, he arranged for additional money from his army salary to be sent to her. Uncle Richard was able to observe *Erev Rosh Hashanah* in Oran, but just a few days into the *Yamim Nora'im*, the High Holy Days, the 48th Engineering Battalion embarked onto the "Durbin Castle," the ship that brought them to a harbor at Bagnoli, just north of Naples, Italy, where they debarked via ferries.[8] This area of Italy had been taken from the Germans by the American army only a few days earlier. The 48th's entrance into World War II began as they joined the US Fifth Army.

The German army had set up a defense line just south of Cassino, including Mt. Porchia. On October 18, 1943, the 48th was transported to just outside of the small town of Caserta, north and slightly east of Naples. Uncle Richard's platoon in the Able Company, led by Lieutenant Orville Munson, received the first job assigned to the battalion: removing mines from a road leading north of Caserta toward the German defense line. By November 22, the feeling of the coming battle started to heat up as German air raids began. The battalion began to bolster their air defense and prepared for potential fighting. Casualties in the 48th had begun. The next day, Uncle Richard's company had to deal with air raids, scrambling into foxholes. Later that day, the 48th was trucked to the hottest battle spot in Italy, near Colli. The battalion weathered an artillery barrage, again hinting at the intensity the US Fifth Army was about to face.

Over the next few weeks, the 48th kept pushing their work further north, constantly repairing bridges, building new bridges, or most often culverts, to make way for the army's vehicles, including tanks and infantry trucks, as they assaulted the German's positions. By December 13, the US Fifth Army had chased the Germans out of the small town of Mignano, which was much closer to the mountains holding the key German defense line. The road the army had to pass would go by Mount Lungo, then Mount Porchia. German military presence on those mountains exposed soldiers using the highway to an awful wide range of gunning. This was the valley the Americans had to pass through to take Cassino.

It was the highway the 48th Engineering Battalion started to work on constantly on December 13. It had been a railroad track the Germans destroyed, so the Allies could not use it. The 48th was ordered to have six miles of the road ready within six days despite

German control of the last four miles. Uncle Richard's company was assigned the job of constructing a series of culverts and some bridge repairs. Every time the Germans saw 10 or more soldiers working on the road, they shot an artillery barrage. Every night the Germans broadcast on the radio that they would successfully hold onto Cassino and the surrounding country.[9]

On December 18, the Able Company started working on another road obstacle, a large railroad bridge that had been blown apart except for partially standing piers. It needed to be fixed and converted into a bridge for army vehicles. They needed bulldozers to clear out the spaces for the embankments, plus they were lowering the level of the bridge to make it easier. This required sometimes working for 36 hours, getting almost no sleep. The noise of the bulldozers caused constant artillery shelling from the Germans. What made the work even harder were constant rainstorms. At one point, the commander, Lieutenant Munson, called the headquarters to tell them he had to bring the men back after 20 hours of continuous shellfire. Because of the rain, the soldiers had to carry many of the new bridge pieces through quagmire-type ground. Yet, despite the constant rain and barrages, Uncle Richard's company got it done quickly.[10] The 48th Battalion got the entire road job done within six days. After the completion on December 21, the battalion got a special commendation from the head of the 5th Army. In a letter to Nana written on December 27, Uncle Richard told her about this assignment, its complications, the shelling, and that he survived.

The direct Allied attack on Mount Porchia began on December 24, with a heavy artillery plastering of the Germans stationed there. Christmas Day for the 48th Battalion was pretty miserable, as there was a strong storm combining heavy winds of almost hurricane level, plus constant heavy rain. The soldiers' pup tents were ripping apart, causing the rain to soak their cots. While Uncle Richard wrote about this difficulty to his sister, he actually did receive a "Christmas present," paperwork confirming his official United States citizenship that began legally on October 31. It must have increased his commitment to fighting for the United States while the 48th Engineering Battalion was ordered to get ready to participate in the attack on Mount Porchia. The infantry casualties in the Fifth Army had been so high that the engineering battalions were getting prepared to join the infantry for the unfolding battle.

The new year of 1944 arrived. On January 3, tank attacks began on Mt. Porchia, with Uncle Richard's company assigned to clear the mines out of the field the tanks would have to cross and to build trails for their approach to the mountain.[11] They ran into a particular problem as some of the Fifth Army's vehicles got stuck in a streambed, and the Able Company was struggling to get them out. This was just a small part of how badly the attack on Mt. Porchia began for the Fifth Army.

The commander of the 48th met with his officer staff on January 5 to let them know the engineering battalion was ordered to take positions in a weak spot next to Mt. Porchia, at the edge of Mt. Maggiore, to confront a possible German counterattack. They set up and manned machine guns, which Uncle Richard had experienced during World War I and was part of his duty in the engineering battalion. The next day, the 48th was relieved of their assignment as infantry so they could return to engineering and repair damage the Germans had done on the highway they had just finished constructing. However, by late afternoon, their assignment was reversed once again.[12] They had to return to roughly the same spot as the night before. The Able Company was attached to the 3rd Battalion of the 6th Armored Infantry, the division that was about to attack Mt. Porchia.[13] The role of the 48th Engineering Battalion in the battle was about to explode.

Mt. Porchia was not a large mountain, only 930 feet high. But the slope, which the Americans needed to climb in the attack, was steep and rocky, providing an easy, natural environment for the Germans to defend. There were only a few places with the kind of paths the US soldiers could use to climb for the attack. The field in front of the slope was very open and easy for the Germans to hammer with all sorts of artillery and gunfire while the Americans crossed it.[14] At dusk, the Able Company began its move to support its assigned battalion. The captain who was the normal commander of the company had fallen ill, so Uncle Richard's platoon commander, Lieutenant Munson, was put in charge of the whole company.

As the Able Company started to move toward Mt. Porchia, many were worried about their lack of battle experience. Most of them were prepared for military engineering. Munson sent Sergeant Buckley to speak to them, which he did calmly and softly, helping to calm some of the soldiers.[15] As one of the few soldiers with combat experience, Uncle Richard was nervous like everyone, but was focused on doing whatever was necessary to defeat the Germans. He had a sense of the type of confrontation that was about to happen. They started moving through the open field under cover of night, but even in the darkness, German artillery fired. All the soldiers hit the ground for protection.

The barrage stopped. The company got up and rushed toward the path they needed to ascend the hill. Sergeant Buckley and three men were leading the company, and one of them stepped on a mine right at the beginning of the path, injuring all three of them along with Sergeant Buckley. Lieutenant Munson then took the lead. They settled in a spot at the bottom of the mountain by 8 p.m. and were sent a command to rush up to attack when they heard the guns firing above them. The firing started at 11 p.m., and the Able Company began to move up the hill, hiding behind rocks to protect them from enemy fire, but so far, there was none pointed at them. Just as Lieutenant Munson got close to the top of the hill, flashes from the Germans' machine guns and rifles lit up the night. The soldiers scattered in different directions to find protection under rocks and behind trees. The company became somewhat spread apart, some closer to the top than others. They continued slowly up the hill. Each time they made a sound, the Germans opened fire again.

Lieutenant Munson made it to the crest of the hill and radioed the rest of the company to get up as fast as possible. Meanwhile, at a lower spot on the mountain, a German officer who spoke fluent English called out to some Able Company men that he wanted to speak to their officer. The only officer there was a lieutenant from the armor infantry battalion. He left his cover and went toward the German officer to speak to him but was shot and killed by the German officer.[16] The company was now stuck, trapped by a range of German weapons, rifles, mortars, and machine guns along the path up the mountain.

During the night of January 6 into the 7th, numerous German soldiers stood on rocks shouting, "American swine!" throwing grenades at any American responders.[17] It was clear the Germans were winning, as most of the armored infantry battalion was gone, with only the 48th Engineering Battalion left on Mt. Porchia. As the sun was rising, Lieutenant Munson took some of the men back to the bottom to pick up more grenades and ammunition to bring back to the top. As dark came that evening and they started back up the hill, Germans would shout questions in English to try and get them to reveal their positions, but Munson commanded his men to be quiet.

Uncle Richard was among the soldiers with Munson. At one spot were two enemy machine gun squads blocking the way to the summit. Uncle Richard stood up in the line of fire and spoke to them in German, referring to them as "comrades" since he served in their army during the First World War. He succeeded in getting both sides to stop shooting. Uncle Richard told the German soldiers they would be surrounded and killed if they did not surrender. He tried for a couple of hours to convince them, but the German soldiers started to shout he was a "swine" and a "traitor," then opened fire. Uncle Richard remained erect, shouting in German to try and get them to stop shooting until his commander ordered him to get down. Then he dropped behind some rocks for protection.

For a stretch, Lieutenant Munson became separated from his troops. As they were crossing a small knoll, a German threw a grenade at them, and he sustained a small injury. The flash of the grenade momentarily blinded him, and he was surrounded by German soldiers. He shouted a warning to his men, then hit the ground and pretended to be dead. The Germans kicked him and took his gun. He did not move, as he was being watched by German machine gunners waiting to shoot at soldiers coming to get him.

Uncle Richard was with the closest Able Company troops trying to reunite with Lieutenant Munson. They opened fire at the Germans in order to get through to him. They became completely surrounded by German machine gunners and had to hit the ground as the shooting intensified. There was fear among them that the only way out was either to be captured or killed. Uncle Richard decided to try once again. He ran to the very center of the line, calling out in German and English for all the shooting to stop. Somehow, he convinced the Germans to halt their shooting. During deep darkness in the middle of the night, he once again stood up erect in the woods, a mere 10 yards from the German machine gunners, and began to speak. "Comrades," he said, "give us our officer, and you will live." The Germans did not answer. Richard continued, "There is no sense in fighting. You are overpowered. Those of you who want to return to the Fatherland alive will come out with your hands up."

After a long stretch of silence, a voice finally answered, "We are willing to give up. What shall we do, bring our guns with us?"

"No, come out in a single file and with hands up," Uncle Richard replied.

Six German machine gunners then surrendered. One of them, an Austrian, told Uncle Richard that two Nazi officers had Lieutenant Munson and they should go after them and kill them. At that moment, German mortars began to shoot, so the acting leader of these Able Company men had them get down to the bottom of the hill to turn in the prisoners and get safe. They escaped the shelling only because Uncle Richard's bluff had convinced the machine gunners blocking their path to surrender. He marched the prisoners to the bottom of the hill.

Lieutenant Munson had not been taken captive by German

officers. Once the shooting stopped, he picked up a carbine left near him and started walking down the hill. He crossed a brook and found two unarmed German soldiers who he took as prisoners and finally reunited with his company. The bulk of the fight for Mt. Porchia was over a day later, as fresh infantry attacked the mountain and finished the battle the 48th Battalion of Engineers had worked so hard to win. A Presidential Citation praised the 48th for the combination of engineering work done under heavy fire in addition to their participation in the battle for Mt. Porchia. Uncle Richard's contribution to the victory was about to be rewarded.

Early in the evening on January 10, 1944, Nana was ironing clothes when the doorbell rang. When she answered, the man asked if she was the next of kin to Richard Stern. Nana began to panic and cry, thinking she was about to be told of his death, but the man was a reporter for the *New York Herald Tribune* and told her the report of Uncle Richard's heroism. He wanted to get personal background information about him to include in the article he was writing. Nana was in such shock that she forgot to turn off the iron until she smelled it burning through the ironing board. The article was published the next morning, not only telling of his heroism but his background as a German-Jewish refugee. It included what was known about some of his family still stuck in Europe. This was just the first stage of Uncle Richard's enormous honor and publicity.

For the next few days, Nana witnessed reactions to the story. Numerous other papers, starting with the *Aufbau*, a German-Jewish paper, published stories. She supplied family pictures to the *New York Daily Mirror* for their article. Many people were calling Nana or stopping her on the way to and from work to congratulate her. She actually took a day off from work to calm down from the combination of her fear for Uncle Richard and her pride in what he did.

Dad had reentered the army on December 29, 1943, this time training in Camp Blanding, near St. Augustine, Florida. Nana sent him copies of the articles that kept appearing and wrote to him how the family always knew Uncle Richard would be putting his life on the line for his friends and relatives. He was now a hero for all the Jewish people. Nana got letters from Jewish organizations congratulating her brother's bravery.

There were several reports about him on the radio. The most famous version actually occurred on April 23, 1944, on station WJZ. It was a dramatic presentation of Jewish soldiers, and the role of Richard Stern was played by Joseph Schildkraut, who was already a famous actor. In 1937, Schildkraut won an Oscar for playing Capt. Alfred Dreyfus in the film *The Life of Emile Zola*. In the 1950s, he would play Otto Frank in both the stage and film versions of *The Diary of Anne Frank*. Uncle Richard's story was told again as part of a portrayal of New York heroes on the radio seven months after it happened on the station WNYC. The United States War Department asked Nana for background information on Uncle Richard in July of 1944 to use his full story as part of publicity to help successful prosecution of the war.[18]

While his friends and relatives in New York celebrated Uncle Richard's bravery and his new status as a celebrity, life for Uncle Richard was still in the middle of the war. While the Fifth Army had taken Mt. Porchia, they were bogged down in making progress against the overall German defensive line preventing them from taking the town of Cassino. The Able Company was constructing more culverts in freezing winter weather. As January unfolded, Uncle Richard was promoted to sergeant. His commander, Lieutenant Munson, was being consulted on how to address a problem in the Rapido River preventing tanks from crossing to attack key German locations. This was another place of a bloody battle. There were walls built in the river holding the water level too high for tanks to cross. Lieutenant Munson organized Able Company's destruction of those walls. When the soldiers of a tank company were nervous about knowing where to cross, Uncle Richard volunteered with another soldier to go ahead of the tanks to get them to the right place under the shelling of German artillery. He was not celebrating. He was fulfilling what he knew was his obligation as a Jew and an American soldier.

By the end of January, Uncle Richard had been recommended for the Distinguished Service Cross, the second-highest medal given for gallantry. His company commander, Lieutenant Munson, wrote one of the letters supporting that medal, stating, "His work is instant, willing, bold, and aggressive." He also said Uncle Richard was a man of excellent character. The report from the 48th battalion said Uncle Richard's calm, thoughtful actions helped his company escape complete destruction and/or being captured. On March 27, 1944, Uncle Richard received the next highest military award, the Silver Star, along with a letter directly from General Mark Clark, who was second in command of the US Army in Europe right under General Dwight Eisenhower. Clark's letter ended with this summary, "Sergeant Stern's coolness and presence of mind under fire enabled his company to continue its advance."

I turned eight years old just as school ended in 1962. Dad then took me on a special father-and-son trip to a friend's lake house in Ontario, Canada. While we drove from West Virginia to Canada, Dad told me stories about serving in the army during World War II. To my surprise, he told me about Uncle Richard's part of the war and how he won the Silver Star. I had never dreamed that he had even fought in World War II, let alone know he was a hero.

A few weeks later, our family did its annual trip from West Virginia to New York, stopping in Allentown to visit Uncle Richard. When we arrived at his house, I ran inside shouting, "Uncle Richard, can I see your Silver Star?" He quietly took me to the back bedroom where I usually slept. His desk was there, and he opened the bottom drawer on the right. He took out a pile of books and folders. At the very bottom of the drawer was the box with the Silver Star. I wanted to ask him why it was hidden, not displayed, but somehow, I was so shocked it was hidden, I could not. He took it out, handed it to me, and said, "Jackie, if you want it, I will give it to you when you are older." I have it.

Richard Stern as sergeant (late January 1944)

AG 220.5-AD   **MAR 27 1944**

Subject: Award of Silver Star.

To: Sergeant Richard F. Stern, 32527983,
           Company A, 48th Engineer Combat Battalion,
           A. P. O. #302, U. S. Army.

        Under the provisions of Army Regulations 600-45, you are awarded
a Silver Star for gallantry in action.

CITATION:

        "RICHARD F. STERN, (32527983), Sergeant, Company A, 48th Engineer
Combat Battalion. For gallantry in action, on 7 January 1944. During
an assault on Mt. Porchio, Italy, Sergeant STERN and other members of
his company were pinned down by enemy machine gun and rifle fire. A
complete enemy encirclement seemed imminent. Sergeant STERN stood
erect in full view of an enemy machine gun nest, and addressing the
Germans in their own language, demanded that they surrender. The machine gunners refused and resumed their fire, but Sergeant STERN stood
erect under fire until ordered to take cover. Later in the engagement
the forward elements of the company were ambushed, and several men were
wounded. Seeking once more to save the situation by ruse, Sergeant
STERN ran into the center of the contested area, shouting to the enemy
and to his own men to cease fire. He then persuaded the enemy troops
that they were surrounded, and further resistance was useless. At this
point, six members of the ambush party dropped their weapons and surrendered. Sergeant STERN'S coolness and presence of mind under fire enabled his company to continue its advance. Entered military service
from Corona, New York."

                                    MARK W. CLARK,
                              Lieutenant General, U. S. Army,
                                     Commanding.

                              -1-

*The Silver Star awarded to Richard Stern with the letter from
General Mark Clark (March 27, 1944)*

_____

1. We the 48th, p 10
2. Idem, p 11
3. Idem, p 13
4. Ibidem
5. Idem, p 20
6. Ibidem
7. Idem, p 21
8. Idem, p 24
9. Idem, p 40
10. Idem, p 45
11. Idem, p 59
12. Idem, p 65
13. Ibidem
14. Idem, p 66
15. Idem, p 67

16. Idem, p 71
17. Idem, p 76
18. Letter from War Department to Martha Romberg, July 6, 1944.

10

SERGEANT STERN

Dad was back in the army, officially entering on December 29, 1943, and beginning his basic training a second time on January 10, 1944. He was having some chest pains from the workouts in the spring and had complained about them in a letter to Richard. On May 1, he wrote a reply from a military camp on the coast of Italy near Mt. Massico. He assured Dad the pain from the heavy exercises would pass but told him to be sure all of his symptoms were noted in his military file. His bottom line was for Dad not to worry. He then told him that the week before, their battalion had a big parade and celebration, in which he received his Silver Star. Two of his friends got Bronze Stars and their commander, Lieutenant Munson, got the Distinguished Service Cross. What he did not share was how this felt like a relaxing break from months of intense engineering work under the pressure of battles.

Through the months of February, March, and April, the Fifth Army launched attack after attack on the German army in Cassino, but they were constantly driven back. One problem was the tank companies not wanting to use what the Able Company had set up for them to cross the Rapido River. So, for a number of weeks, there was no productive use of tank-born artillery in attacking the

German units in Cassino. Part of the problem was the Fifth Army overall was small, and the 48th Engineering Battalion's soldiers were being stretched thin. One of the saddest events was the death of Sergeant Buckley, who had been injured in the attack on Mt. Porchia. He was the person who had calmed the nervous unit members. He recovered from that injury and returned to the company but was killed in one of the continuous barrages the company suffered through their constant assignments on the front lines. Richard's company collected 400 dollars to send to Buckley's wife, who was carrying a baby about to be born.[1]

On March 15, Able Company began construction of two bridges over the Rapido River. The company was commanded to complete the second bridge during one night, March 18 to 19, under constant shelling by German artillery. A flare would be shot up, then the shelling would start.[2] The soldiers would stay still, and when the flare dimmed, began working again. Despite the constant barrage, the bridge was completed that night.[3] By March 24, the 48th Battalion had been in nonstop battle situations, whether constructing or fighting, for one hundred and four days.[4] The Able Company felt frustrated and exhausted. They were relieved when they were finally pulled out of the front lines to be given a chance to rest. On April 10, they went to the camp near Mt. Massico, where they did experiments with new equipment. They also built a jeep trail up the mountain.[5]

The 48th Engineering Battalion rejoined the Italian campaign by mid-May. Throughout the month, the Fifth Army had much better success, moving north quickly with the goal of taking Rome away from German occupation. The Able Company did a myriad of jobs, from sweeping minefields to fixing roads to working on bridges. There was one horrifying incident that reminded members of the 48th of the terrible reality of war. They were sent into a town that had been occupied by the German army and was bombed by Allied planes. Units from the 48th were to check out the town, be sure German soldiers were gone, and get any useful information. One platoon was shocked upon finding a church that had been converted into a hospital, with a Red Cross on its roof. Inside were over 50 dead people, all civilians, including women and children. All had been killed from the bombing by Allied planes.[6] They sadly saw how bombs do not just fall on armed fortifications but often kill innocent civilians.

Beginning on May 27, 1944, Uncle Richard's company was in six different locations as the battle against the Germans was pushing forward quickly. On June 5, the Fifth Army entered Rome upon defeating the German army. The 48th Battalion was one of the official military occupiers of Rome until June 20, when they were sent back to Naples to prepare for their next campaign. Their training camp was about 20 miles south of Salerno, where they practiced for the next six weeks on how to do a beach invasion. It was clear they would be confronting the German army at a southern beach of France.

One of the key functions of the 48th was learning how to demolish undersea obstacles.[7] That must have tipped off Uncle Richard on what was going to be the next campaign, even though it was not his role. Having been a frontline machine gunner in World War I, one of his primary duties was to organize machine gun protection for the Able Company during engineering assignments, so he participated in new machine gun training. In a letter Uncle Richard wrote to Dad on July 29, he gave a heads up that Dad should not expect any regular mail or even to hear from him for the next few months. He wrote the same to Nana so she would not worry. It was also clear that Dad was fully healthy again, as Uncle Richard told Dad he was happy to hear things were going well.

The 48th boarded a boat on August 10 to assist the attack on the "Red Beach," but the initial assault did not go well, so they were redirected to land on the "Green Beach," which had been taken by the 141st Infantry Division on August 11.[8] This location was at St. Raphael, France, a coastal town that had been occupied by the German army. On August 12, the 48th, along with another engineering battalion, took over the occupation of St. Raphael to search for hidden German soldiers and find any information the Germans left behind.

Uncle Richard, now a sergeant, led one of the squads that searched the town. On August 15, he found an abandoned German headquarters that had a map of all the minefields, pillboxes, and gun positions for miles around the Yellow Beach. He, of course, could translate all the notes, and when this was turned over to the commander of the infantry division leading the fight on the Yellow Beach, he was thanked for this extremely valuable information. Over the next two days, the Able Company took on the assignment of deactivating one of the mine locations and blowing up two of the pillboxes.

The 48th Battalion was reassigned to the 7th Army on August 21 and began a quick journey through southern France. Over the next five days, they traveled more than one hundred miles, passing through French towns with the residents standing outside and cheering the Americans, offering fresh fruit and wine along with throwing kisses and saluting the soldiers. By August 27, the Able Company was working on fixing a bridge at St. Julian, then proceeded to Grenoble.[9] Over the next 12 days, they went toward Baume-Les-Dame, where the French Underground only a few days earlier had a disastrous confrontation with the German army. The 48th saw a mass funeral for many of the civilians the Germans killed as part of their action against the underground, as well as the "thank you" to the Americans as their army units arrived and forced the German army out.[10] By early October, the 48th was near Eloyes, France, very close to Alsace, which is where Uncle Richard spent some of his time fighting for the German army 26 years earlier.

In a letter to Nana from October 30, Uncle Richard shared a humorous story that illustrated his confidence in Nazi Germany's pending defeat. His company was working in a forest in France, and one of his buddies was cutting down a tree. Someone patted his buddy on the shoulder. His young friend turned around, and four Nazi soldiers who deserted the German army were standing behind him. Despite their inability to speak English, they made every effort they could to be clear they wanted to be his prisoner. The young friend, who Richard called "the boy," was so scared, "his trousers became heavy for the time being," but he recovered and completed cutting down the tree. The new prisoners carried the tree trunk down to the road for him. These four German soldiers clearly felt it was better to surrender to the American army than to risk being killed in a battle. For the past several weeks, one of my uncle's responsibilities had been to oversee German prisoners captured by his company, which is how he was able to help his young friend.

In early July of 1944, Dad wrote to Uncle Richard about how he was still waiting to be assigned to an army unit headed to Europe. He had been trained as an anti-tank gunner. Finally, toward the end of the summer, he was assigned to the 103rd Infantry Division, known as the "Cactus" Division. They had been activated during the summer of 1942 but spent two years reorganizing and training. Dad mentioned in a September 10 letter to Uncle Richard that he still had no idea when his unit would go overseas.

It was in a letter Dad wrote to Nana on September 11, 1944, that Dad expressed new optimism and hopes for the family. He wrote this about the defeat of Hitler, "The mortal enemy of mankind will have to bend and bow before us." Because he felt that was inevitable, he added that the family would soon be together again. He wished Nana a *Shanah Tovah* (happy new year) for the Jewish year of 5705. On October 5, 1944, the Cactus Division finally left the United States, landing in Marseilles, France, on October 20. The division was moved north in France very quickly. By November 9, they were in Docelles, which was in Alsace, about 40 miles from Uncle Richard's battalion. As it turned out, within several days, the Able Company worked overnight, creating a bridge that the Cactus Division needed to cross. It was a bridge they worked on silently at night, as it was so close to the German lines that they were in danger from mortar shelling. During the war, army units could sometimes be almost right next to each other but still never know it. Dad, with some of his comrades, saw trucks with what looked like the emblems of Richard's battalion on them but was unsure.

On November 11, Richard's company was not on the front line, so he took the time to write a long letter to his family in New York. He began by praising all of the items sent to him by friends and family. He shared them with his unit and said how much it was appreciated. The family knew Belgium had been freed from Germany and had asked about the Flogerhovers. Uncle Richard replied that he had written to Thekla a long time earlier but had not heard back. He also mentioned he knew his unit was very close to Dad's division.

One very rainy morning, November 20, Dad was cleaning an anti-tank gun and heard someone say, "Private Rudi is over there." He looked up. Walking through the mud and the rain was Uncle Richard, carrying a carbine on his shoulder and crying from happiness as he approached Dad. Uncle Richard knew his company had built a bridge for the Cactus Division and found them. He then asked where he could find his nephew, the young man he had raised from a small child, and who he had not seen for over two years. A soldier who knew Dad pointed him out. They were thrilled to spend the bulk of the day together, having lunch, exchanging their army experiences, and comparing news from the family. Dad had not yet participated in a serious battle, so Uncle Richard shared a lot of insight into the different shelling and bombing sounds, trying to make Dad more aware of how to protect himself in different circumstances. Just before leaving to return to his company, Uncle Richard, who in Jewish tradition was a descendent of the priesthood, placed his hands on the helmet Dad was wearing and blessed him with the *Bircat haCohanim*, the Priestly Benediction, from Numbers Chapter Six:

"*Y'varechecha Adonai v'yishmarecha,*
Ya'eir Adonai panav eilecha vechuneka,
Yisa Adonai panav eilecha v'yasem l'cha shalom."

"May God bless you and keep you,
May God's face shine upon you
and be gracious to you,
May God's countenance shine upon you
and give you peace."

For the rest of his life, Dad felt that it was Uncle Richard's blessing that got him safely through the war. His division was at the edge of the Battle of the Bulge but not struck too badly. Dad did participate in some difficult battles, but nothing like Uncle Richard had experienced in Italy.

After they crossed into Germany, the division commander, because of Dad's fluent German, used him as a translator to speak with inhabitants of the towns to find commanding headquarters, which included getting the German occupants out of the home. In one town, Dad saw a beautiful home he felt was great for the commanding officers. He met the woman who owned it, who pleaded with him not to take it, saying her family were not Nazis. Dad told her they had 10 minutes to leave the home, and when he walked by her into the next room, he saw a large photo of Hitler on the wall and other Nazi symbols. He went back and told her they had five minutes to leave. Another time he found a house with barrels of beer in the basement, so he tasted the beer from each barrel, claiming to be testing them for his commander.

A few weeks after Uncle Richard and Dad saw each other, the 48th Battalion finally got a period of rest after 113 days of constant engineering duties and combat. Uncle Richard shared a number of thoughts with Nana through a letter written on December 11, 1944. He knew his company was still fairly close to Dad's division and had hoped to see him again at a service for the first night of Chanukah, December 10, but he had an assignment and could not attend. He congratulated Nana on getting her US citizenship and was pleased to learn she was in good health. He wrote a lot about how he appreciated that the family back in New York was constantly sending him packages with items like salami, coffee, cigars, and candy. He was sending money back to Nana to save, since he did not want the family to spend so much on items for him, especially the cigars. What he enjoyed the most was coffee, which he liked to mix with cognac. He claimed that calmed his nerves. What he wanted them to always send, however, was candy, but not for himself. He explained how the soldiers would give candy to the poor children they constantly encountered.

The Allied armies took Belgium away from Nazi Germany in September 1944. As a result, Uncle Richard and the rest of the family were finally able to receive a few letters from his sister, Thekla, who updated them on her family's situation. During the summer of 1944, as the Germans were now clearly losing the war, they began to gather mixed married couples in Belgium the way they had previously gathered to imprison Jewish couples. The Flogerhovers fled to a family in the countryside that was supposedly friends. They were clearly not comfortable housing Thekla and her family, so the Flogerhovers only stayed for a short time. When they went back to Brussels, they were able to stay safe because the Nazi army had become more focused on surviving the fight with the Allies.

Once Belgium was freed, the government arrested anyone that had been a German citizen who could well be a Nazi. So by late fall in 1944, Heinz Flogerhover ended up in prison, as he had accidentally spoken in German to officials instead of in Flemish. Uncle Richard knew about this and wanted to get some time off to go to Brussels and testify on Heinz's behalf. He felt it was important to tell them about Heinz's support for his protest against the Nazis in 1933. However, as the 48th Battalion was deeply involved in battles, he could not get time off. He ended up writing a letter testifying on behalf of Heinz, but he kept hoping to go and testify in person. In his December 11 letter to Nana, he shared the news of Heinz's arrest. Uncle Richard knew that since Heinz was Catholic, not Jewish, he was suspected of being a Nazi German. He expressed his hope for the war to end soon, so he could begin to search Europe for any surviving family. Having gone over two years with no information about the bulk of family members who never got out of Europe, he was desperate to find and try to help them.

The last major offensive by the German army, the Battle of the Bulge, began on December 16, 1944. Dad, in the Cactus Division, was at the edge of the battle, not directly attacked. Uncle Richard's battalion, as part of the 7th Army, was in the center of a particular sub-campaign of the Battle of the Bulge, Operation Nordwind, launched by the Germans on December 31, 1944. The 7th Army was forced to retreat from its advanced position, and the 48th Engineering Battalion was sent to defend the headquarters of the army around Saverne, France, while the commanding officers withdrew to a safer place. On New Year's Day of 1945, Uncle Richard had to do exactly what he did on New Year's Day of 1944, set up defensive machine guns. By mid-January, Operation Nordwind had been contained enough that the 48th battalion was taken from the front lines and transferred to a location to teach new engineering battalions how to operate on the front lines. Able Company's assigned focus was teaching about erecting bridges. During this time, Richard felt no worries, being confident it was just a matter of time before the war would be over. He also finally began to write his letters in English.

On February 8, 1945, the 48th Battalion entered Germany for the first time, occupying the town of Ludweiler. From their arrival until March 10, they stayed stationed in Ludweiler as front-line infantry, not as engineers. Part of their role was sending out squads to find German army positions and sometimes to confront them. As a sergeant and machine gunner, Uncle Richard took part in a number of these squad missions. After their month in Ludweiler, the 48th returned to engineering duties, and on March 18, they crossed the Saar River in Germany. The Able Company built a bridge and then sent troops into the nearby town to check for German soldiers. By March 28, they crossed the Rhine into Bavaria. The journey to the war's end was quickly approaching, and Uncle Richard's assignments became less constant, so he could start focusing on his concerns for family survivors.

By early April, numerous German divisions began surrendering to Allies on the eastern and western fronts. Uncle Richard was able to leave for Brussels on April 8, traveling over 200 miles to be with his sister Thekla, her husband Heinz, and their daughter Ellen. Thekla was shocked at his presence, thinking he must have been too active in the Allied offensive to be with family. He finally learned about their full experience under Nazi rule for the past five years.

He let the family in America know his sister did not look bad, and he spoke highly of her daughter Ellen, who spoke French and English fluently. More important, since Heinz had been arrested by the Belgium government, under the suspicion of being a German citizen, Ellen did a lot to support her mother, including a job that earned enough to feed them and take care of basic needs. Uncle Richard instructed his family in New York to start shipping the Flogerhovers coffee, soap, and pepper in one-pound packages, as well as clothing, stating that Thekla and Ellen could swap with others if something did not fit properly. He was determined to do everything possible to help the family he had finally found.

He spent two days running with Thekla and Ellen from one Belgian official to another, getting the paperwork together for Heinz's release. When meeting with the minister of justice, Uncle Richard made a sworn statement attesting to who Heinz truly was and taking responsibility for him. He was convinced the justice minister now had no case with evidence against Heinz. On April 11, his last day in Brussels, Uncle Richard went to visit Heinz in the internment camp near Antwerp. He pledged he would provide an affidavit so the Flogerhovers could immigrate to the United States. Heinz was finally released on April 26, but Uncle Richard did not know his brother-in-law was free until June.

Sadly, Uncle Richard began to learn about the fate of other family members and friends. He met a female cousin who had been hidden for years while her husband had been taken to the Mauthausen concentration camp, where he was shot in November 1942. He met his friend Josef, whose wife and son had been deported and killed. He had learned at the end of 1943 that his brother Heinrich had likely been sent to Auschwitz, but no one had heard from him since 1942. His brother Heinrich's wife, Frieda, and daughter Elisa had been slaughtered by the Nazis. He still had not heard exactly what had been Heinrich's fate. Uncle Richard's first cousin Irene Cossman had divorced her husband and moved to the United States in 1934. Her ex-husband was also killed. Her mother, his Aunt Frieda, Uncle Leopold's wife, had been deported and murdered. His Uncle Leopold had died of cancer on March 31, 1942, in the Cologne Jewish hospital.

He learned some of this when he stopped in Cologne on April 11, on his way back to his battalion. During this first stop in Cologne, he found no evidence of any living family other than those he already knew about. He only learned of deaths, as well as seeing the total destruction of his longtime home city, including his home on Marsilstein that had been destroyed by Allied bombing. While waiting to cross the Rhine River, he just missed Dad's company by about five minutes. He wrote a short note to Dad and gave it to a captain of his division to deliver. He wanted Dad to begin learning about their family's fate.

Not all family issues Uncle Richard handled were tragic. With the war clearly heading to its end, he was asked to deal with numerous matters. A great example is another version of one he commented on in 1940, when his cousins Henni and Carl Katz did not approve of their son Michael marrying Ilse. In the spring of 1945, it involved Dad getting engaged via mail to a woman in New York. His mom objected to this and wrote to Uncle Richard how, at 22 years old, Dad was too young to get married. Nana referred to him in a diminutive German word that means "young boy." She added that he must not truly be in love, but just desperate for a relationship with a girl because of being in the army overseas. Just like Uncle Richard encouraged Michael Katz to go ahead and get married, stating his parents were stuck in an old-school approach, he wrote Dad his "heartfelt best wishes" for the engagement. He had the opposite of Nana's view, writing that if he married young, Dad would not regret it because "each man is the architect of his own happiness." There is little doubt that Uncle Richard wanted Dad to enjoy a better life than himself, since at age 46, having spent so much of his life dealing with suppression and resulting problems, he was still not married. He did not want his sister Martha's narrow-mindedness to direct Dad's life. I was surprised to learn Dad was engaged in 1945. I only knew about him meeting my mom in 1952. She told me Dad was engaged a total of three times!

After Uncle Richard returned to his company on April 11, his main job was to help oversee the German prisoners taken by his battalion. He assisted in screening and determining the positions that each prisoner held. After they were assigned a company to help with construction work, Uncle Richard carried the bulk of the load of managing prisoners because he was the only soldier in the Able Company who was fluent in German. He had a German-Jewish friend in Company C, Ernest Breiner, who did the same for his company. They would talk about how much they wished they could take revenge on Nazi prisoners and how much they should really care about providing their food and clothing, but they had to follow the rules laid down by the Allies concerning prisoners. Just after the war in Europe was officially over on May 8, Uncle Richard was taking part in screening a thousand new prisoners. They discovered two of them were SS soldiers, identifying them through the blood type tattoos most SS troops had under their left upper arms. He referred to them as SS dogs.

In the middle of May, both Dad and Uncle Richard ended up in military hospitals. The Cactus Division had taken control of Innsbruck, Austria, on May 3. So, just after the war ended, Dad took a couple of days off to go skiing in the Alps and ended up with an injury—breaking his leg the weekend of May 11. Uncle Richard wrote to Dad in the hospital on May 24, offering a healing prayer, then on May 27, he ended up in the hospital with malaria. He recovered in about a week and kept in contact with Dad, telling him he should be patient with his recovery and plan on visiting the Flogerhovers in Brussels once he had healed.

On June 14, 1945, Uncle Richard submitted a request for a furlough or to delay his travel to the port where he would board a ship to take him back to New York. There were four reasons he listed: to visit his sister and her family in Brussels; to visit Dad in the hospital in Reims, France; to go to the graves of his parents in Cologne, Germany; and to search Cologne for any information about 25 of his relatives, including his brother Heinrich, stating specifically he had not heard from him since 1942. He was granted the furlough beginning June 20. In Cologne, Uncle Richard was able to visit his parents' graves. As he researched family, he learned that everyone on his list was dead. This included the fate of his brother. In a letter to Dad, he described the emotion as only finding graves, not lives.

Learning about the murder of Heinrich Stern in Auschwitz dramatically illustrates the parallels and differences between his and Uncle Richard's lives. Their parallels were starting retail businesses with their father, Markus, and serving the German army in World War I. Their differences include Heinrich's joyful volunteering for the German army as a Jew determined to prove his dedication to the fatherland. This reflected the positive attitude for World War I by the general German public when it began. Richard was drafted and saw his service in the army as a patriotic obligation, similar to his forefathers who served during the wars of 1812 and 1870/71. While both served on the front lines, Uncle Richard was the decorated soldier.

When the Nazis took power and began their persecution of German Jews, Jewish front-line war veterans had respect from many of their non-Jewish German comrades who had served with them. This helped Jewish war veterans think the rein of the Nazi Party would be limited—another parallel between Heinrich and Uncle Richard. But their difference was Uncle Richard was a protester, using his status as a war veteran to make his key points. Heinrich was completely quiet. The depression of all German-Jewish war veterans deepened with the passing of the Nuremberg Laws and the Military Service Law from 1935, reaching a horrifying stage at *Kristallnacht*. After *Kristallnacht*, Heinrich took his wife and daughter to Belgium, Uncle Richard saw the United States as the best possibility for his sister Martha and her son as well as himself. Once in America, his newfound freedom helped inspire him to find a way to oppose the Nazis once again. That inspiration pushed him to volunteer for the American army. He saw it beyond getting revenge, but in helping any family member he could. Heinrich's end was the common tragic death of European Jews. Uncle Richard's was to serve in a way that led to heroism.

By the beginning of July, Dad's leg was pretty well healed, and he decided to go to Brussels to finally visit his Aunt Thekla, Uncle Heinz, and cousin Ellen. He arrived at their house on July 11, his 22nd birthday, and Uncle Richard was already there. This surviving part of the family was able to spend a few days exploring the city, imagining what it would be like once the Flogerhovers joined the rest of the family living in New York. Dad felt this family reunion was the highlight of his military time in Europe.

Uncle Richard was honorably discharged from the army a few weeks later, on August 10, after arriving back in New York on August 6. By September, he was working once again in the textile industry as a screen maker for Renee Screen Studios. He was a union member earning sixty dollars per week. On November 26, 1945, he received the affidavit from the US government in which he pledged his assets to support Thekla, Heinz, and Ellen once they arrived in America. He then mailed the affidavit to the American Consul General in Brussels, along with a letter pleading for visas to be given to them. He gave his history as a decorated American soldier and closed the letter with these words, "As the above named relatives are the only ones left, it is my only wish to have them here with me. I am single, have no dependents, live in a three-room apartment, and earn enough money to support my relatives at any time." The Flogerhovers, the only relatives he found alive at the end of the war, arrived in America on December 2, 1946.

It is easy to see Uncle Richard's service in the US Army as exceptional. Not only did he win the Silver Star, but he proved to be an invaluable asset, fully dedicated to fighting the German Nazis and proud to do it as an American soldier. He deeply appreciated the more respected way he was treated in the US Army versus the German army. Whatever his commanders needed, he did, often as a volunteer, since he was looking for the meaning in life he felt was lost when his protest against the Nazis failed in Cologne on April 1, 1933. He fulfilled his desire to stand up and oppose Nazism. Uncle Richard wanted to get revenge on behalf of the Jewish people, for his family, and for the loss of civil rights that resulted from the rise of a dictatorship. Despite the medal for his bravery, for all the publicity he had earned, and the ultimate defeat of Nazi Germany, a cloud of deep disappointment, of sadness came to him at the end of the war. It did not dominate his living, but it hung with him for the rest of his life. I believe it was from one of his last experiences just before Germany surrendered.

On April 29, 1945, the 45th infantry division of the 7th Army liberated the Dachau concentration camp. The 48th Engineering Battalion went to see Dachau on May 1, the day of the inmates' celebration of liberation, led by Rabbi David Eichorn. Uncle Richard saw the piles of dead Jewish bodies in parts of the camp. He saw how thin and denigrated the victims were and began to work bringing food and clothing to the survivors. Once he learned his brother Heinrich's fate, Dachau showed him exactly what Heinrich must have suffered. His friend serving in the Charley Company, Ernest Breiner, was also a German-Jewish refugee who had been imprisoned in Dachau for three months in 1937. Breiner found only two of his cousins among the survivors. His father had been killed, along with so much of his family. Uncle Richard sent Dad a pile of pictures, taken by US Army photographers, of dead bodies, liberated prisoners, and various details of Dachau. He told him he had to keep those photographs, along with an urn from the camp's crematorium. Uncle Richard then wrote, "don't ever forget, or our joint fight was in vain." His words were a critical, eternal teaching. Purpose in life exists only through your personal commitment, which you must maintain. For Uncle Richard and Dad, it was the evil of National Socialism that inspired their moral convictions. Both opposed this kind of cruelty until the end of their lives.

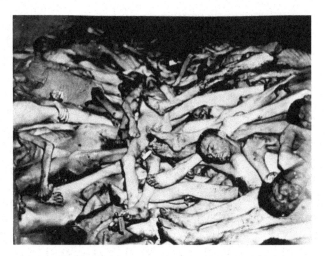

What Richard Stern saw when his unit entered concentration camp Dachau the day after it was liberated

Heinrich Stern, the oldest sibling of Richard Stern (1940)

Richard Stern and Rudi Romberg in Brussels (July 1945)

Richard Stern along with Rudi Romberg visiting Richard's sister Thekla, her husband Heinz and daughter Ellen in Brussels, Belgium (July 1945)

---

1. We the 48th, p 103
2. Idem, p 116
3. Ibidem
4. Idem, p 118
5. Idem, p 119
6. Idem, p 152
7. Idem, p 165
8. Idem, p 170

9. Idem, p 179
10. Idem, p 189

11

A HEART ALWAYS OPEN

Uncle Richard fought for Germany in World War I for a year and a half, lived over six years under Nazi persecution, and then served for three years in the American army. So, by age 46, Uncle Richard hoped for a quiet, peaceful, drama-free life. While he felt he was too old to raise children of his own, he desired a marriage to go along with his financial stability. He wanted to enjoy the family that had survived Nazism and made it to the United States. He wanted to see Dad succeed in his cabinet-making career. He loved hosting gatherings for family and friends at his apartment in Queens. Despite experiencing a dramatic, sometimes devastating life, those who socialized with him noted he never lost his sense of humor. Uncle Richard had some wonderful moments in the last 22 years of his life, but he also had to keep dealing with family members' problems, personal conflicts, and serious health issues.

After Dad returned from Europe fully recovered from his broken leg, he was hired as a cabinet-maker by a furniture manufacturing company in New York. He became a member of the Furniture Workers Union and motivated his fellow workers to unionize their factory. He only worked there for a year. In 1947, he started his own small cabinet shop in Queens, New York. The business began well, and he moved to a larger factory in Manhattan in 1948. As a factory owner, he ended up in conflict with the union that he had helped organize. Later that year, Uncle Richard became a partner with Dad in his furniture company, Kos-Rom Modern Furniture. Uncle Richard handled all of the needed paperwork, dealt with customers, did bookkeeping, took care of bills, searched for better-priced materials, and did some work in the factory if Dad said it was needed. Dad often repeated a lesson he learned from Uncle Richard during this time—that the cost of the materials used to construct the furniture had a bigger impact on profits than the selling price.

February 22, 1949, was Uncle Richard's 50th birthday. Dad wrote a poem that encapsulated the feelings Richard had about his life. For example, Dad wrote it was a pity my uncle had not married because he would be "the most marvelous" husband and, for a baby, the "sweetest father." Dad also praised all of Richard's accomplishments in the army and as a protester against the Nazis. But most notable was Dad's observation that he was the best sibling and the most affectionate uncle. His poem described Richard this way, "A heart always for others, it was a heart full of humor, a hand always open and an ear always open." Dad felt bad for Richard because not every family member appreciated him.

Shortly after his birthday, Uncle Richard met the woman he would marry, Hilde Seligmann. She fulfilled his largest desire, to increase his happiness with life. Hilde was considered a true Jewish "Cologne woman," as she was born in Porz, Germany, a small town just outside of Cologne. She made it to America in 1937 and worked in sales for Loft's Candy. They got married on September 4, 1949. In a poem written for that occasion, she was described as the person making the "star" (a translation of Stern) a blessed man. Hilde was 15 years younger than Uncle Richard. He often referred to her as *meines Täubchen*, "my little dove." While they would not be able to have their own children, the marriage had finally fulfilled the desire for a partner in life.

My parents got married on February 22, 1953, Uncle Richard's 54th birthday. Around the time I was born, May 30, 1954, Dad was making some significant changes in his furniture manufacturing and worked out a business separation with Uncle Richard. This was necessary because, in 1955, after negotiating with Fairmont's economic development authority, Kos-Rom was absorbed by a group in Fairmont, West Virginia, and renamed "Fairmont Furniture." The same year we moved to Fairmont, Uncle Richard and Aunt Hilde began negotiating with Hilde's first cousin, Richard Mathis, about becoming involved in his business in Allentown, Pennsylvania—Table Supply Meat Market.

Mathis and his partner, Mia Indig, had been running the market for a few years. It expanded from just a meat market to a full grocery store, including fresh produce. Mathis told Uncle Richard they needed someone to take over the produce and grocery segments, so he could focus on the meat market. Uncle Richard decided to buy the produce and grocery departments of the store at the market on South 4th Street in Allentown. Per his contract, he paid half of the monthly rent plus twenty-five dollars per week toward joint advertising in local newspapers and a radio station. Mathis and Indig were supposed to include Uncle Richard as their co-tenant in any negotiations for rent renewal. In addition, they were obligated to let him know of any information affecting the store. Uncle Richard officially purchased his part of the store at the end of July 1956. The store's name was Table Supply.

Some of my earliest memories of Uncle Richard were from stopping at the market to say hello to him when we arrived in Allentown for our visit before continuing to New York. I would run into the store, ask where Uncle Richard was, and usually go back to the produce area. He would give me a big hug with a happy smile and then hand me some silver dollars he'd collected for me between our visits. After I looked through their different styles and dates, Mom took them to keep safe and later put them in my coin collection.

I also remembered Richard Mathis, and even more, his wife Frieda Mathis, who was much younger than him. They had met and married a few years following the war after she immigrated to America. Frieda had been a prisoner in the Auschwitz concentration camp. She was one of the young women that Dr.

Josef Mengele submitted to torturous medical experiments. Frieda was always very sweet and kindhearted. She would take extra food from the Table Supply store and donate it to places that fed the poor. She was a generous donator to charities throughout her life. As a little boy, I did not know about her experience in Auschwitz, even though I was curious about the tattooed number on her arm. I was told she could not have children, although she always enjoyed being with young children, such as my younger brother and me. My memories of Richard Mathis are not like Frieda. At five and six years old, I did not know any details about him, but I always thought he felt a bit creepy. That instinct turned out to be correct, confirmed years later when I learned about what he tried to do to Uncle Richard.

At the end of October 1956, Mathis and Indig opened a second store also named "Table Supply" on Walbert Avenue in Allentown. For the first two weeks, they only sold meat. Then they added produce and groceries, causing a large loss of business for Uncle Richard. He still paid his obligations. According to their business agreement, he was going to file the name "Table Supply, Stern Grocery and Produce Department," which would show the connection between what Uncle Richard owned and what Mathis and Indig owned, but the attorney who was supposed to represent all of them never did it. Uncle Richard ended up going to court himself to file the name. It turned out Mathis had instructed the attorney not to file the name. Then Mathis and Indig tried to stop Uncle Richard from selling canned meats that had been part of the grocery department before Uncle Richard took it over, which was confirmed by Frieda Mathis, as a witness. It was clear Mathis and Indig were greedy and upset by the success in sales Uncle Richard achieved in a short time.

Even worse, Mathis and Indig engaged in a new lease negotiation with the owner of the South 4th Street building, signing a five-year agreement increasing the rent and presenting Uncle Richard with a new sublease raising his rent. They claimed the owner had insisted on the conditions of the new lease. However, the owner and his attorney testified that was not true.

Further, Mathis and Indig never informed Uncle Richard of what they were doing. Their next step was to open a third store in Hellertown, a small town just south of Allentown's twin city, Bethlehem. They insisted that Richard pay one-third of the advertising costs for all three stores, even though he only ran part of one store, plus they created produce and grocery segments in the other two stores to compete with him. All of this was a violation of the original business agreement made in July of 1956. Their intention was to have him pay more of their costs as they opened additional stores in competition with Uncle Richard's segment of their original store.

In October of 1959, Richard filed a legal complaint in the Allentown peace court, claiming that Mathis and Indig's actions broke the original agreement. The peace court ruled in Mathis and Indig's favor. He then filed a lawsuit in a superior court that ruled in his favor. This legal confrontation went all the way to the Pennsylvania Supreme Court, which ruled in Uncle Richard's favor on May 23, 1961. Sadly, Richard, within a year after getting a favorable ruling, decided to retire. At age 62, he had already been experiencing heart troubles for over two years. The pressure put on him created by Mathis and Indig quickened the decline of his heart's health. A friend of his in Miami Beach told him he should move there, but Uncle Richard preferred to stay in Allentown. Fortunately, he had built and still owned a successful business. His wife, Hilde, being much younger, kept working there until they decided to close it a few years later. In 1963, he started to receive income as a US veteran in addition to some reparations from Germany.

Early in 1959, Dad made a trip back to Germany to investigate better machinery for the furniture factory in Fairmont. Uncle Richard gave him the name of an old friend in Cologne who had a lot of knowledge of the furniture industry. He also told Dad to visit the family's graves and look into getting any new family information. He clearly meant about the Stern and Katz families. Dad, however, ended up meeting Oskar Romberg, the only one of his father Walter's eleven siblings who survived in Essen, Germany, through most of the war. His second wife, who he married in 1932, was Catholic. She worked at a church, and the priest would hide Oskar whenever the SS was looking for him. In early 1945, he was captured and sent to Theresienstadt. He was one of the few still there and liberated by the Russians on May 1, 1945. He returned to his wife in Essen. Oskar was also involved in the furniture business. Dad met one of his youngest daughters, Anne, who was only eleven years old and learning English because she wanted to study in America for a while. Dad and Anne exchanged a couple of letters, the only connection Dad had to the Romberg family until the end of the 20th century. He did not discuss this very much with Uncle Richard to avoid any arguments over the Romberg family.

The summer of 1959, after I turned five, was the last time Dad and I stayed overnight in Nana's apartment while in New York. As usual, she made the pudding I loved. I had no idea she was already struggling with an illness that turned out to be cancer. By February of 1959, Nana had been feeling sick for a while. Uncle Richard gave her constant attention, either talking to her by phone or taking a bus to New York to be with her. He pushed her to check into Memorial Hospital for tests. That is when she learned it was cancer and started radiology treatment. In April, she wrote a will, knowing she would probably not live much longer. It was clear at that time she still did not care for my mom, as she wrote this in the will, "my last wish is that all assets handed over are strictly personal to Rudi, and not used in or at the private household."

Uncle Richard spent a few days with Nana in early August while Hilde was taking a vacation in the Poconos with some friends. He let Dad know she was not feeling well. Nana was supposed to get radiation treatment every day and stay in the hospital, but she felt it was too depressing to be with suffering people all day long. Instead, she went for longer treatments three days per week. One time, when Uncle Richard accompanied her, he noticed how slowly she walked and how long it took just to get to the station where she caught a subway to the hospital. He also went with her to an appointment with a surgeon who scheduled brain surgery for her. Nana really preferred to go back to Allentown with her brother, as he provided the most comfort.

By the end of November, Nana could no longer walk up and down stairs, so it was impossible to use a subway for transportation. She was forced to either take a taxi or a car sent by the Red Cross. Richard would get to New York as much as possible to help her go to and from hospital treatments. As the intensity of her pain continually increased, he kept Dad informed. By the end of 1959, she rarely kept any food down, generally because of the radiation treatment. At that point, Richard said Nana's destiny was in the hands of God and her strong willpower. I remember seeing her in the hospital once during her last six months alive, but I am not sure of the date. During those last months, she told Dad how wrong she had felt about her treatment of Mom.

For Richard, losing another sibling on May 16, 1960, was devastating but was not the end of his emotional suffering caused by family issues. He was the sibling who constantly tried to resolve family arguments. In letters he had written while serving in the American army during World War II, there were plenty of references to unwarranted family confrontations. For a stretch, Nana was arguing with her sister Hilda and brother-in-law Ludwig. Uncle Richard would write to them that family is indispensable. He urged them to stand together, especially since they were experiencing hard times. One time, he was so concerned about a family argument that he placed a long-distance call from training camp, even though he literally only had thirty cents in cash at that moment.

After Nana's death, another conflict arose. This time, there were arguments between Hilda and Ludwig Walker versus Thekla and Heinz Flogerhover, who all lived in New York. Apparently, the Walkers were accusing the Flogerhovers of doing something completely wrong, possibly illegal, but Uncle Richard said they should not be spreading this around, given they had no proof. In a letter to Dad, he did not describe the issue, just said not to get involved in the argument. More devastating was the unknown death of his sister Thekla.

On his 64th birthday, Friday, February 22, 1963, he got an unexpected call from Heinz. After he wished Uncle Richard a happy birthday, Thekla got on the phone but could not seem to talk fluently. Uncle Richard told her to rest. He knew she had been dealing with health issues and said he would come to visit her after the weekend. However, the weather got nasty with a snowstorm, so he did not make the trip until the following Thursday. He arrived at her apartment at 4:30 p.m. but got no answer. He thought she must be in the hospital. He called a mutual friend, Paula, who did not know where Thekla was and came over. Uncle Richard then called Thekla's older daughter Ruth. When he asked where her mother was, she answered coldly, "We are coming straight from her funeral." Paula took the phone from him and spoke to Ruth for the next several minutes. He sat frozen for a while, not understanding why neither of her daughters told him his sister had died the day before. He returned to his home in Allentown and did his own *shiva* (a service of prayers to mourn the loss of a loved one) for Thekla. He now felt completely separated from the Flogerhover family, who he had helped in Belgium and arranged to bring to America. He never received any reason why Ruth and Ellen did not tell him of his sister's death, despite all the help he had given their family.

In December of 1963, 20 years after the beginning of the ferocious battle on Mt. Porcia where Uncle Richard won the Silver Star, he sent a Christmas card to his battalion's commander, A. J. Goodpaster, who was now a major general. Goodpaster wrote a lovely letter in return, stating how there was no part of his long service in the military that had any more meaning to him than that campaign in Italy. He remembered Uncle Richard very well.

When we moved to Allentown, I noticed how Uncle Richard was slowing down. When he took us on our first walk to the Allentown Fair, he began secretly dropping coins for Len, stopping and saying, "I shmell money!" as he had done for me. Sadly, I could see how he was struggling physically.

Not all of my observations were sad. I could tell he and Mom had become much closer, as he often told Dad that Mom was right and he should listen to her. He loved when Mom could be the person driving him someplace he wanted or needed to go. He enjoyed having his "grandsons" living so close to him and was excited when Mom became pregnant with her third child in 1965. Like the rest of us, he thought and hoped Mom would have a daughter. I really wanted a sister and knew my parents would name her Karen. What was sad, however, was Uncle Richard's declining health.

On December 18, 1965, the first night of Chanukah, we received this letter from Eliezer ben Mordechai haCohen, supposedly the Chanukah Man.

Dear Romberg Brothers,

Your Uncle Richard, may God bless him another twenty-five years, wrote a letter several weeks ago to me, and was telling me about you two boys. You both were, during this last year, fairly good, and I should make it my business this year, and come to visit Allentown.

Sorry I can't make it, because this year I have to go to Russia and Siberia to bring the poor Jewish children some goodies. Enclosed I send you some money, and your Mami can buy something in Hess's Bargain Basement.

Also, I heard the good news that your Daddy and Mami ordered a custom-built brand new baby girl, but your Daddy put the order in too late and the delivery cannot be before the end of January 1966. Let's be with mazel tov, and we will later celebrate, whatever comes out.

Good Chanukah, yours,

Eliezer ben Mordechai haCohen.

Here was the return address on the envelope: 4711 Matzah Ball Street, Tel Aviv, Israel. Uncle Richard was very ill, yet still clever.

At eleven years old in sixth grade, I knew this was from Uncle Richard and thought it was funny. On January 19, 1966, Len and I did not get a sister Karen, but our youngest brother, Barry.

As I entered junior high school, I became less attentive to family. I was enamored with a cute girl in my homeroom and more focused on trying to be a well-liked class member. I did not interact much with Uncle Richard, as he was struggling with his health, and I was too centered on life with my peers. He did tell me how he expected me to be the first family member he knew to enter college. As I was preparing for my bar mitzvah, our rabbi told me I should think about becoming a rabbi. The rabbi also often told me he thought I looked like Henry Fonda. Uncle Richard thought it would be great for me to want to be a rabbi but definitely did not think I looked like Henry Fonda. Despite my lack of interaction with him during my seventh-grade year, he was very proud of my bar mitzvah on May 27, 1967.

In December of 1967, the middle of my year in eighth grade, Dad was in the hospital for a hernia operation. Mom took me to visit him. In Dad's room, she told me that Uncle Richard was also in the hospital, dealing with his heart problems once again. She asked if I wanted to see him. I did, so we went up to his room. When we walked in, Uncle Richard looked up, saw me, and started to cry. I saw how sick he was, and I had no idea what to say. I went over to his bed and told him I hoped he felt better. He hugged me, not with the strength he usually did, and kept crying. When we left, I asked Mom why he cried. She answered, "I think he doesn't want you to see him so weak." In spite of how little time I had spent with him during the past year, Uncle Richard knew he was my hero.

Three days later, on December 22, 1967, he died. My parents took me with them to the Jewish cemetery in New Jersey, where Uncle Richard would be buried. They did not let me walk through the cemetery to the burial at his grave because of their superstition that I was too young to walk where dead people are buried. They left me alone in the car. I wanted to be at the graveside to say goodbye to Uncle Richard. By 13 years old, I had started to learn how exceptional his life had been. I regretted I could not sit with him to hear the details of his experience. Even more, I felt grief that my youngest brother, Barry, would never get to know the Chanukah Man.

Richard Stern's marriage to Hilde Seligman (September 4, 1949)

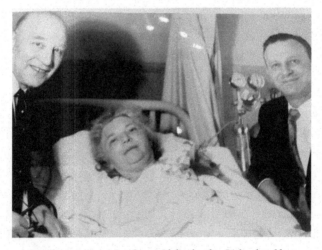

Martha (née Stern) Romberg with her brother Richard and her son Rudi in hospital, a few weeks before she died (1960)

Richard Stern dressed up as the Chanukah Man with Rudi Romberg and Len and Jack Romberg (December 1963)

EPILOGUE

As a child, I loved TV shows and movies about World War II. Every week I watched *Combat!* I thought heroism was either fooling enemies or standing up against them in a battle. When I heard about Uncle Richard winning the Silver Star, he fulfilled my model of a hero. By eighth grade, I was learning a lot more about the history of the Holocaust. I had seen the picture of Uncle Richard standing in the doorway of his store next to a Nazi SA officer in a book written in German about the history of Jews in Cologne. I never had the chance to talk to him about that picture, so I did not know right away about his protest. I was a teenager when I learned about his service as a German soldier in World War I and how he used his status as a veteran to protest against the Nazis. I knew he loved our family but did not know the details of his dedication to the much wider family I had never met or even realized existed. In college, I studied German history, and that is when I would have many conversations with Dad about Uncle Richard's life and his connection to German history. By the early 1970s, Dad began to do some speaking about our family's experience in Nazi Germany. He kept pushing Uncle Richard's lesson to him about not forgetting the reason they fought in World War II by repeating that we must stand up against persecution from white supremacists.

I thought a lot about Uncle Richard as a young adult. I had seen some of his documents, the original copies of newspaper articles about how he earned his Silver Star, and a pile of letters Dad had in German. In the early 1980s, Dad met with the mayor of Cologne and convinced him to invite Jewish survivors back to Cologne for the *Karneval*. That started a series of trips to Cologne for Dad and Mom when they made a number of new friends in Germany. Most notable was Dieter Corbach, who often taught German teenage students about the Holocaust. Corbach invited Dad to be a guest speaker for classes, and of course, he talked a lot about Uncle Richard. Dad provided Corbach with a pile of information and copies of pictures and documents about Uncle Richard's story. That enabled him to write a short book in German for students called *Ich kann nicht schweigen!* (*I cannot be silent!*), which was part of his larger project, *Spurensuche jüdischen Wirkens* (*Searching for Traces of Jewish Action*).

In 1991, when Rodney King was beaten by Los Angeles policemen, Dad called me in tears, saying it made him feel like he was back in Germany. Dad felt that African Americans were being treated in the United States like Jews were in Germany. This was a reminder of the parallels between the history of German Jews from their emancipation onward and African Americans from their liberation from slavery and their living through the Jim Crow era. Despite laws from the time Bismarck was the German prime minister through the Weimar Republic, antisemitism ran deep in Germany. From the aftermath of the Civil War to today, racism has remained deeply embedded in the United States.

I entered rabbinic school at age 42, after spending 18 years in business. When it was time to give my senior sermon, I utilized a part of Uncle Richard's story for the first time. That week's Torah portion, *Vayeira*, began with Abraham sitting in the doorway to his tent while recovering from his adult circumcision. He welcomed and fed three strangers. The subject of the sermon was our responsibilities while being in the doorway of our residence, and I connected this to the reason Uncle Richard stood in his doorway in 1933, with the Nazi SA officer standing next to him. Numerous times over the years as a rabbi, I have used stories from Uncle Richard's life to make a key point.

For years, I did not get Uncle Richard's Silver Star. His wife, Aunt Hilde, had it and I never asked for it. When I became ordained as a rabbi, Dad gave me a special present. He put together a framed piece of work that contained the famous picture of Uncle Richard protesting in his doorway, a picture of him in the German army, the certificate awarding him the Iron Cross, a picture of him as a sergeant in the American army, the original letter from General Mark Clark awarding him the Silver Star and the actual Silver Star. Dad had told Aunt Hilde it was time to fulfill the promise Uncle Richard made to me when I was a child. Uncle Richard would have agreed that I was old enough to receive his Silver Star. I always kept that framed piece illustrating a short version of Uncle Richard's history, hanging in my rabbinic office. Whenever I encountered something difficult, I looked at his pictures to remind me I had nothing of difficulty to deal with compared to his life.

Corbach's work ended up getting Uncle Richard's picture in various museums in Germany, with a large version along with a picture of his anti-Nazi pamphlet in the Jewish Museum in Berlin. It is in the beginning section of the museum that tells the story of the Jewish people when the Nazis took power. When I saw that museum in 2012, I had been told the picture was in the museum but had no idea it was so largely displayed. I stood still, staring at it for at least 10 minutes, unable to move, comment, or totally absorb its prominence in the museum. That moment reinforced the idea that I had to fully research Uncle Richard and get as much of his story together as possible. Dad had died in 2008. I just wished he could have been with me to see that display.

In August of 2011, our family was found by the Romberg family survivors, most of whom Dad never knew existed. Many of them were his first cousins, the children of his father's siblings. The only ones he had actually met were Anne and her father from Essen, Germany. It had taken members of the Romberg family decades to learn who survived and to find each other. We were the last ones found. One of Dad's first cousins who he had never met, Bert

Romberg, organized a family meeting in Dallas for all possible members. I helped him and got to know Bert rather well. The Romberg family members were all wonderful. The stories of the different family groups were fascinating and often inspiring, but the more I heard, the more I realized Uncle Richard's story was unique.

Mom moved out of their home to an apartment in 2017. She had boxes of picture albums Dad had put together. Many of the pictures were not relevant anymore, but I took all of the boxes home to look through every album before throwing any pictures out. To my surprise, in one of the boxes were all of Uncle Richard's letters, documents, poems about him, newspaper articles about him, the original protest pamphlet from 1933, plus so many more informative items, including his service booklet from World War I. As I got the letters and other items in German translated, I learned so much about his life and how he kept trying to help so many family members and others through hard times. When I went to Germany to collect more information about the Stern family's history, I ended up meeting Michael Vieten, who wrote a book on the Katz family that Uncle Richard's cousin had joined through marriage. He gave me another chunk of letters written to and from Uncle Richard.

As I researched Uncle Richard's life and compared it to a number of stories, I had also learned about the Romberg side of the family's history. I saw a number of cases in which Christian Germans who served with Jews in World War I helped their veteran comrades even under Nazi rule. Professor Michael Geheran's book, "Comrades Betrayed," confirmed this was part of the history leading to the Holocaust.

In elementary school, I believed a hero was someone who served in a war. As a teenager and in college, I learned a hero was someone who stood up for civil rights, including standing up for oppressed people when their own life was put in danger. After reading over 60 letters involving Uncle Richard and his relatives, I realized that a hero is also someone who addresses the needs of family regardless of how it affects him or her personally. When

Uncle Richard took responsibility for his sister Martha and her son, my dad, his personal life changed in many unpredictable ways. Under Nazi rule, even when fearful for his own life, he did what he could for family in addition to harboring Jews fleeing from Austria and trying to just get away from Nazis. His dedication to his oldest sister and her family was placed before insuring his own personal financial saving. His attempts to keep family from splitting over silly dramatic situations were important in times of tension. Perhaps most important were the lessons he tried to teach his family, not only about opposition to the fascists but simply putting the needs of others before your own. The doorway to heroism did not simply bring Uncle Richard to find it in a war or a protest, but moral heroism in everyday life.

ACKNOWLEDGMENTS

There are many people I need to acknowledge and thank for their assistance in my research, translation of German documents and letters, providing additional items and editing. My first translator was Gabriela Maduro, who was recommended to me while she was a student at Florida State University. She began in the summer of 2018 and translated a number of typed letters. I needed someone who could at least begin to translate the handwritten letters. For that, I thank Michael Harris.

I was very fortunate to be unexpectedly contacted by Bob Bendix, a son of my dad's cousin, Ellen Bendix née Flogerhover. He sent me a copy of a short piece his mom had written about the history of the Flogerhover family. This gave some great insight into Uncle Richard's sister and her husband, in particular while they lived in Belgium.

Once I retired in June of 2019, I knew it was necessary to travel to Germany in order to conduct research in Cologne and in Weilerswist. I am very fortunate to have a close relationship with my cousin, Anne Romberg, who lives in Essen, Germany. I must thank her for many helpful roles. First, she helped me find and set up contact people who worked in municipal archives and museums. Anne also told me she would work on translating handwritten letters, so I mailed a batch to her before traveling to Germany. Once there, she drove me to Weilerwist and was my interpreter with people who did not speak English. When I showed her Uncle Richard's military service booklet from World War I, she introduced me to Franz and Margret Dissen, who were German history experts, especially on the German army. They translated the booklet for me and shared some additional military information.

In Weilerswist, I met with the town's archivist, Dagmar Theissen, who not only provided me with information on Uncle Richard's father, Markus, but took me to the house Uncle Richard was born in, gave me a tour of the Jewish cemeteries and the location in Freisheim where Seligmann Stern built a house and a synagogue. She also provided a picture of the house and a photo of the original drawn plan of the house and synagogue. She also arranged for Helene Kurten, the author of a book about the history of the Jewish community in Weilerswist and Freisheim, to be with us and provide all of the information I have on Seligmann Stern.

In Cologne, I did research in the Cologne archives, the Roonstrasse Synagogue, and the EL DE Haus Museum. In the Cologne archives, information was gathered by the director, Ulrich Fischer, and his associate Jan Klein. They provided information on the homes and businesses of the Stern family. After I returned home, Mr. Klein sent an email with a lot of helpful information. The EL DE Haus Museum tells the story of Nazism in Cologne. It is located in the building that was the Gestapo's office and prison. One of their historians, Birte Klarzyk, provided a lot of historical information about the Jews of Cologne, took care of some translations, confirmed Uncle Richard's uniqueness and shared some important pictures. She stayed in contact with me, always helping when I needed clarifications or additional information.

I offer special gratitude to Esther Bugaeva, who works for the Roonstrasse Synagogue. She not only provided information on the Stern family and the history of the Roonstrasse Synagogue, but she introduced me to Michael Vieten, who wrote the book about the Katz family. Ms. Bugaeva stayed in touch with me constantly, confirming and searching for information about Stern family and friends when I requested it. Thanks to her, I spent a great afternoon with Mr. Vieten, who provided me with a copy of his book and emailed me copies of 14 letters written by Richard Stern plus four written to him.

In New York, I met with Dr. Frank Mecklenburg, the head archivist of the Leo Baeck Institute. He provided me with historical insights, an article and recommended Dr. Susan Ray as a translator who handled all of the letters shared by Mr. Vieten as well as a large number of letters and writings uncovered in the fall of 2019. I thank Gary Yorden for helping with chapter titles.

I give special thanks to Benay Stein, a professional editor. She provided editing and thoughts for the first draft of my manuscript. I learned a lot from her during the process.

Lastly, I give my greatest thanks and love to my mom, Ellen Romberg. Through my numerous conversations about Uncle Richard and our family, she shared a number of things I did not know, confirmed what I remembered from childhood, and even translated a couple of items for me.

BIBLIOGRAPHY

Bormann, Heidi and Cornelius, *Die Landjuden in den Synagogengemeinden Gymnich, Friesheim und Lechenich*, Stadt Erftstadt, Kerpen, 2nd edition, 1994

Bracher, Karl Dietrich, *The German Dictatorship. The Origins, Structure, and Effects of National Socialism*, Praeger Publishers, New York, Washington, 1970

"Cologne During National Socialism," written for the EL-DE Haus Museum, NS Documentation Center, Cologne, Germany

Corbach, Dieter, "'Ich kann nicht Schweigen!' Richard Stern. Köln, Marsilstein 20", in: *Spurensuche jüdischen Wirkens - 2*, Cologne, Scriba, 1988

Craig, Gordon A., *Germany 1866-1945*, Oxford University Press, New York, NY, 1978

Elon, Amos, *The Pity of It All. A History of the Jews in Germany, 1743-1933*, Metropolitan Books, New York, NY, 2002

Kurten, Helene, "Haus Heskamp, erbaut around 1900," in: *Weilerswist 700 years 1310 - 2010. History and Homeland Association of the Community of Weilerswist e.V.*, Weilerswist village community, Verlag Ralf Liebe - Edition Landpresse, Weilerswist, 2010, pp. 144-160

Rheins, Carl J., "Deutscher Vortrpp, Gefolgschaft deutscher Juden," in: *The Leo Baeck Institut Year Book*, Volume 26, Issue 1, January, 1981

Thalmann, Rita and Feinermann, Emmanuel, *Crystal Night*, Coward, McCann & Geoghegan, Inc., New York, NY, 1974

United States Army, "We the 48th" in: *World War Regimental Histories*, 1945

Vieten, Michael, *Katz-Rosenthal, Ehrenstrasse 86, Cologne*, Heinrich & Heinrich, Berlin, Germany, 2017

Letter about Richard Stern's internment at Geschwister Wolff from December 2, 1916

Three letters written by Heinrich Stern

Two letters written by Elise Stern

Document turning over ownership of bedding store to Richard Stern from Markus Stern from December 29, 1927

Multiple letters by Richard Stern

Multiple letters by Martha Romberg (né Stern)

Multiple letters by Rudolf Romberg

Military service booklet from World War I of Richard Stern

Certificate awarding the Iron Cross 2nd Class to Richard Stern on August 22, 1918

Original protest pamphlet written by Richard Stern in 1933

Multiple poems written to honor Richard Stern, two when leaving Germany, one for 50th birthday, one for his marriage to Hilde Seligman

Will written by Richard Stern on October 26, 1942

Order to Richard Stern to report for induction into the American army from September 22, 1942

Letter to Richard Stern by Major John Scially from October 20, 1942

Letter to Martha Romberg about Richard Stern from the USO December 8, 1942

Martha Romberg's answer to a request from the US army for information on Richard Stern from July 13, 1944

Letter awarding the Silver Star to Richard Stern from General Mark W. Clark from March 27, 1944

Letter to Martha Romberg from United Jewish Appeal regarding the Radio presentation on Richard Stern from April 21, 1944

Request from Richard Stern for delay to return home in order to visit the Flogerhovers in Belgium from June 14, 1945, approved on June 19, 1945

Honorable discharge document from the American army for Richard Stern from August 10, 1945

Affidavit filed with American government pledging money to bring the Flogerhovers over to the United States from November 26, 1945

Ellen Bendix's personal story written about the Flogerhover family

Will written by Martha Romberg on April 11, 1959

Short story of his life written by Richard Stern on June 1, 1959

Recording of Rudolf Romberg's interview with the Spielberg Foundation in 1997

KIND REQUEST

Dear Reader,

If you have enjoyed reading my book,
please do leave a review on Amazon or Goodreads. A few kind
words would be enough. This would be greatly appreciated.

Alternatively, if you have read my book as Kindle eBook you could
leave a rating. That is just one simple click, indicating how many
stars of five you think this book deserves.
This will only cost you a split second.
Thank you very much in advance!

W. Jack Romberg

ABOUT THE AUTHOR

W. Jack Romberg retired as the rabbi of Temple Israel in Tallahassee, FL in the summer of 2019. It was his second career. He intended to enter rabbinic school after graduating from University of Pittsburgh in 1976 with a BA in history focusing on Germany, but his father asked him to help in the family's furniture manufacturing business.

In 1995, he decided to pursue the lifelong dream to be a rabbi, entering Hebrew Union College-Jewish Institute of Religion in 1996, earning a master's degree in 1999 and ordained in 2001. Before retiring, Rabbi Romberg decided to write the book on his great uncle Richard Stern, perhaps forming a third career.

As a rabbi, Romberg was deeply involved in the general community, interfaith programs as well as non-partisan community issues. He did frequent opening blessings at the state legislature, the governor's cabinet meetings, and county commission meetings. He wrote many editorials for the *Tallahassee Democrat*, the local newspaper. In 2008, he served on the paper's editorial board as the chosen community person.

Romberg led these organizations: *The Interfaith Clergy Association*, *The Village Square*, and the *Tallahassee Equality Action Ministry*, and was on the board of the Tallahassee Symphony Orchestra for 15 years.

For a special concert in 2017, that told the story of music performed by prisoners in the Theresienstadt ghetto during the Holocaust, he wrote the narrative, selected the music, and was a narrator in the concert.

He was a frequent guest speaker on local TV discussion shows and a local NPR radio show. At the retirement gala celebrating his role in the city, the mayor presented him a key to the city.

HOLOCAUST SURVIVOR TRUE STORIES

The Series **Holocaust Survivor True Stories WWII**, by Amsterdam Publishers, consists of the following biographies:

1. Among the Reeds. The true story of how a family survived the Holocaust, by Tammy Bottner

Amazon Link: getbook.at/ATRBottner

2. A Holocaust Memoir of Love & Resilience. Mama's Survival from Lithuania to America, by Ettie Zilber

Amazon Link: getbook.at/Zilber

3. Living among the Dead. My Grandmother's Holocaust Survival Story of Love and Strength, by Adena Bernstein Astrowsky

Amazon Link: mybook.to/ManiaL

4. Heart Songs - A Holocaust Memoir, by Barbara Gilford

Amazon Link: getbook.at/HeartSongs

5. Shoes of the Shoah. The Tomorrow of Yesterday, by Dorothy Pierce

Amazon Link: getbook.at/shoah

6. Hidden in Berlin. A Holocaust Memoir, by Evelyn Joseph Grossman

Amazon Link: getbook.at/HiddenBL

7. Separated Together. The Incredible True WWII Story of Soulmates Stranded an Ocean Apart, by Kenneth P. Price, Ph.D.

Amazon Link: getbook.at/SeparatedTG

8. The Man Across the River: The incredible story of one man's will to survive the Holocaust, by Zvi Wiesenfeld

Amazon Link: getbook.at/ZviWi

9. If Anyone Calls, Tell Them I Died. A Memoir, by Emanuel (Manu) Rosen

Amazon Link: getbook.at/EMrosen

10. The House on Thrömerstrasse. A Story of Rebirth and Renewal in the Wake of the Holocaust, by Ron Vincent

Amazon Link: getbook.at/RVincent

11. Dancing with my Father. His hidden past. Her quest for truth. How Nazi Vienna shaped a family's identity, by Jo Sorochinsky

Amazon Link: getbook.at/DancingJS

12. The Story Keeper. Weaving the Threads of Time and Memory. A Memoir, by Fred Feldman

Amazon Link: getbook.at/StoryKeeper

13. Krisia's Silence. The Girl who was not on Schindler's List, by Ronny Hein

Amazon Link: getbook.at/Krisia

14. Defying Death on the Danube. A Holocaust Survival Story, by Debbie J. Callahan with Henry Stern

Amazon Link: getbook.at/Danube

15. A Doorway to Heroism. A decorated German-Jewish Soldier who became an American Hero, by W. Jack Romberg

Amazon Link:

16. The Shoemaker's Son. The Life of a Holocaust Resister, by Laura Beth Bakst

Amazon Link:

17. When the Music Stopped. Willy Rosen's Holocaust, by Casey J. Hayes (forthcoming)

HOLOCAUST SURVIVOR MEMOIRS

The Series **Holocaust Survivor Memoirs World War II** , by Amsterdam Publishers, consists of the following autobiographies of survivors:

1. Outcry - Holocaust Memoirs, by Manny Steinberg

Amazon Link: getbook.at/Outcry

2. Hank Brodt Holocaust Memoirs. A Candle and a Promise, by Deborah Donnelly

Amazon Link: getbook.at/Brodt

3. The Dead Years. Holocaust Memoirs, by Joseph Schupack

Amazon Link: getbook.at/Schupack

4. Rescued from the Ashes. The Diary of Leokadia Schmidt, Survivor of the Warsaw Ghetto, by Leokadia Schmidt

Amazon Link: getbook.at/Leokadia

5. My Lvov. Holocaust Memoir of a twelve-year-old Girl, by Janina Hescheles

Amazon Link: getbook.at/Lvov

6. Remembering Ravensbrück. From Holocaust to Healing, by Natalie Hess

Amazon Link: getbook.at/Ravensbruck

7. Wolf. A Story of Hate, by Zeev Scheinwald with Ella Scheinwald

Amazon Link: getbook.at/wolf

8. Save my Children. An Astonishing Tale of Survival and its Unlikely Hero, by Leon Kleiner with Edwin Stepp

Amazon Link: getbook.at/LeonKleiner

9. Holocaust Memoirs of a Bergen-Belsen Survivor & Classmate of Anne Frank, by Nanette Blitz Konig

Amazon Link: getbook.at/BlitzKonig

10. Defiant German - Defiant Jew. A Holocaust Memoir from inside the Third Reich, by Walter Leopold with Les Leopold

Amazon Link: getbook.at/leopold

11. In a Land of Forest and Darkness. The Holocaust Story of two Jewish Partisans, by Sara Lustigman Omelinski

Amazon Link: getbook.at/Omelinski

Forthcoming:

JEWISH CHILDREN IN THE HOLOCAUST

The Series **Jewish Children in the Holocaust,** by Amsterdam Publishers, consists of the following autobiographies of Jewish children hidden during WWII in the Netherlands.

1. Searching for Home. The Impact of WWII on a Hidden Child, by Joseph Gosler

Amazon Link: getbook.at/gosler

2. See You Tonight and Promise to be a Good Boy! War memories, by Salo Muller

Amazon Link: getbook.at/salo

3. Sounds from Silence. Reflections of a Child Holocaust Survivor, Psychiatrist and Teacher, by Robert Krell

Amazon Link: getbook.at/SoundsX